Yemen and the Politics of Permanent Crisis

Sarah Phillips

Yemen and the Politics of Permanent Crisis

Sarah Phillips

IISS The International Institute for Strategic Studies

The International Institute for Strategic Studies

Arundel House | 13–15 Arundel Street | Temple Place | London | WC2R 3DX | UK

First published June 2011 by **Routledge**
4 Park Square, Milton Park, Abingdon, Oxon, OX14 4RN

for **The International Institute for Strategic Studies**
Arundel House, 13–15 Arundel Street, Temple Place, London, WC2R 3DX, UK
www.iiss.org

Simultaneously published in the USA and Canada by **Routledge**
270 Madison Ave., New York, NY 10016

Routledge is an imprint of Taylor & Francis, an Informa Business

© 2011 The International Institute for Strategic Studies

DIRECTOR-GENERAL AND CHIEF EXECUTIVE John Chipman
EDITOR Nicholas Redman
ASSISTANT EDITOR Janis Lee
EDITORIAL Jeffrey Mazo, James Fidler, Ayse Abdullah
COVER/PRODUCTION John Buck

The International Institute for Strategic Studies is an independent centre for research, information and debate on the problems of conflict, however caused, that have, or potentially have, an important military content. The Council and Staff of the Institute are international and its membership is drawn from almost 100 countries. The Institute is independent and it alone decides what activities to conduct. It owes no allegiance to any government, any group of governments or any political or other organisation. The IISS stresses rigorous research with a forward-looking policy orientation and places particular emphasis on bringing new perspectives to the strategic debate.

The Institute's publications are designed to meet the needs of a wider audience than its own membership and are available on subscription, by mail order and in good book-shops. Further details at www.iiss.org.

Printed and bound in Great Britain by Bell & Bain Ltd, Thornliebank, Glasgow

British Library Cataloguing in Publication Data
A catalogue record for this book is available from the British Library

Library of Congress Cataloging in Publication Data

ADELPHI series
ISSN 1944-5571

ADELPHI 420
ISBN 978-0-415-69574-9

Contents

ACKNOWLEDGEMENTS

There are many who deserve thanks for the completion of this project but first among them is Abdul-Ghani al-Iryani, who conducted the Developmental Leadership Program in my absence, under difficult circumstances. As always, his insightful analysis and boundless optimism were invaluable to the completion of this work; he is a national treasure. Many thanks are also owed to his wife Susan, who hosted me so many times, and made the memorable offer to rush a home-cooked meal to Sana'a airport to see me through my hasty return to Sydney when I was refused entry to Yemen in January 2010.

There are others that I would like to thank wholeheartedly but in the current climate they must remain anonymous. Mrt, m, to (sort of) name but two, you know who you are and I thank you deeply. I would also like to thank those who took part in the DLP survey that informed this study: your generous insights into why efforts had failed to avoid what should have been avoidable were incredibly valuable.

I am extremely grateful to the Developmental Leadership Program for financing this research, and in particular to Adrian Leftwich for his astute judgements and rigour; and to Steve Hogg at AusAID for spearheading such an important project on the nature of donor interventions in developing states. Any remaining errors are, of course, mine alone.

Finally, thanks to my wonderful family (and their rather charming poodle), and to Hamish for prompting me to do things that I pretend I don't want to do but secretly enjoy.

GLOSSARY

ACC	Arab Cooperation Council
AQAP	Al-Qaeda in the Arabian Peninsula
COCA	Central Organisation for Control and Auditing
DFID	Department for International Development
DLP	Developmental Leadership Program
GCC	Gulf Cooperation Council
GPC	General People's Congress
IMF	International Monetary Fund
JMP	Joint Meeting Parties
MCC	Millennium Challenge Corporation
MECO	Military Economic Corporation
MOPIC	Ministry of Planning and International Affairs
PDRY	People's Democratic Republic of Yemen (formerly South Yemen)
PSO	Political Security Organisation
UAE	United Arab Emirates
UNSC	United Nations Security Council
UPF	Union of Popular Forces
USAID	United States Agency for International Development
YAR	Yemen Arab Republic (formerly North Yemen)
YECO	Yemen Economic Corporation
YSP	Yemeni Socialist Party

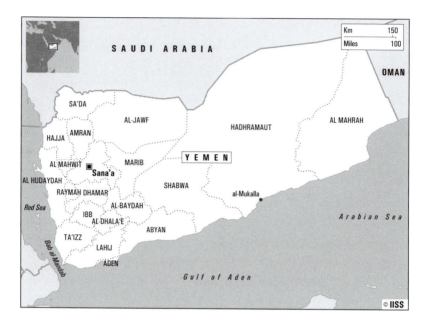

How did it come to this?

The events of early 2011 across the Middle East have given cause for unprecedented hope, but also trepidation, for the future. Following popular uprisings on the scale witnessed in Tunisia, Egypt, Syria, Libya and Bahrain, the natural impulse is to speculate on what transformations may occur, but it is equally important to examine the underlying drivers of the changes that have already occurred because they reveal much about constraints and opportunities for the future. This book looks behind the scenes at the Yemeni regime's opaque internal politics and at the nature of the neo-patrimonial system it has entrenched in the 33 years since President Ali Abdullah Saleh assumed power. As this book went to press, it remained to be seen whether Yemenis would secure the reforms that could revive their economy, or whether parts of President Saleh's regime would cling to power despite the defection of numerous elite supporters, the open revolt of powerful tribes and Saleh's decision to go to Saudi Arabia to seek medical treatment for injuries sustained in an attack on his compound. What was clear, however, is that after the brutal crackdown on unarmed protesters in Sana'a on 18 March 2011, President Saleh had lost the considerable level of popular legitimacy that had hitherto bolstered his regime. In the days that followed, sections of Saleh's inner circle that had been complicit in the criminalisation of the state for nearly 33 years began to publicly defect.

Deeply patrimonial systems of power are not transformed overnight, and many of Yemen's structural and human barriers to developmental change remain in place. The defection of key members of the inner circle to the opposition was not in itself a signal that a more developmentally inclined elite was in the ascendant, although many of the young protesters have been articulating demands for a fundamental revision of the political system. Those who defected from Saleh's inner circle had been instrumental in instilling the dysfunctional political settlement that brought Yemen to this point. By joining the protest movement they have not necessarily committed themselves to a democratic or post-patrimonial future. Indeed, none has gone so far as to openly renounce the patrimonial system of government from which they benefited, or the 'rules of the game' that will shape the behaviour of anyone who might follow President Saleh. Several other factors have a significant bearing on the future of the Yemeni regime: the role of Western and regional actors in enabling the dysfunctional rules of the game to endure; the similarities between the regime and the formal opposition in their preference for closed-door patrimonial bargaining over inclusive participatory politics; and wider questions over how the West can or should engage with crisis states that pose a threat to international security.

The Yemeni system is no stranger to crisis; in fact, crisis has kept the system running, and has been, to a significant degree, a deliberate choice by Yemen's power elite. The regime of President Saleh has chosen not to implement the rule of law despite its capacity to do so. It has chosen not to plan for a post-oil economy despite the possibilities for an investment-based model, and has instead mortgaged its future on its ability to bargain for external support. Finally, it has chosen to reward those who reinforce the legitimacy of a system that endorses the criminalisation of the state. Despite the centrality of crisis to the regime's business model, Western policymakers continue to argue that Yemen must be stabilised – a notion that is increasingly misaligned with ground realities. Yemen, like most of the Middle East, needs change more than it needs the tenuous stability that Saleh offered.

For more than 32 years, the Yemeni system under President Saleh had been remarkably adept at withstanding crises – manipulating their forces to channel them away from the political centre. In so doing Saleh retained power in an environment that would make many dictators dizzy. By appearing to juggle political crises he contributed to the popular belief that the country will collapse into anarchy without him – a perception that has served him well and that he has worked hard to maintain. However, what Saleh's system was not built to withstand is the collective perception that crisis is not necessary, or that crisis is not an unavoidable part of the political process, or that maybe there is another way to conduct the political process. These are precisely the perceptions that began to wash over Yemen's citizens in early 2011, representing an extraordinary shift in the president's fortunes. They have gained support perhaps in part due to the privations that continue to afflict the people: 30% of citizens do not have basic food security, which is defined as unreliable access to sufficient, safe and nutritious food needed for a healthy life.[1] So while the fear of chaos is highly rational, it must be balanced against other pressing needs. As the Arab uprisings have illustrated, beliefs and perceptions of risk can shift much faster than the playbooks of ageing autocrats. The idea that Arab presidents are not necessarily presidents for life was proven by the departure of Egypt's Hosni Mubarak, and the inspiration that this has provided cannot be dismissed by creating more crisis and more fear of the unknown. In finessing his ability to win at the politics of permanent crisis, President Saleh lost the ability to anticipate and plan for change. Perhaps this is why, in early March 2011, Saleh quietly sanctioned the release of 70 suspected al-Qaeda operatives from the Political Security prison in Sana'a[2] – an apparent insurance policy intended to graphically illustrate how dangerous Yemen is. President Saleh has always ruled by creating confusion, crisis and sometimes fear among would-be challengers. Releasing people who can who can create these feelings helps to sustain the belief that Yemeni politics is confusing, chaotic, frightening and better left to those used to handling it.

One of the enduring myths about Yemen is that change has been very slow. At first glance, the men wearing their *jambiyya*, or ornamental daggers, as they walk the streets; the women covered behind a full-face veil; and the near-ubiquitous presence of the mild narcotic *qat*, it appears that this is a medieval society quite impervious to change. Nothing could be further from the truth. Change has been rapid and transformative. Yemeni communities have been connected with new roads, telecommunications technology and satellite television; at the same time, employment in the cities and abroad, and an ever-increasing dependence on world food prices, make Yemen very much embedded in global trends. Yemeni officials often make the point that, despite its apparent instability and relatively low human development indicators, Yemen has in fact seen tremendous development within a short period of time. Just 50 years ago north Yemen was still ruled by a hereditary imam and the country was virtually inaccessible to outsiders. Its public infrastructure, health and education services were rudimentary in the extreme and until 1947, the imam still so valued isolation that he prevented his subjects from leaving the country to pursue education.[3] When the imam was deposed in 1962, the average life expectancy was just 35 years of age. The areas in south Yemen surrounding the city of Aden did not gain their independence from Britain until 1967, and the Republic of Yemen was not created until 1990. It should not be surprising, therefore, that Yemen's formal political foundations are still under negotiation just one generation after they were established.

Yemen's political settlements (the processes by which the balance of power is negotiated between competing elites and social forces) have been hastily forged.[4] In the 1970s and 1980s, north Yemen was largely a subsistence and remittance-based economy. Then, at the same time as almost a million Yemeni workers were expelled from the Gulf as punishment for Yemen's equivocal stance on Iraq's invasion of Kuwait in 1990, the country's oil exports began to increase dramatically. The balance of power rapidly switched from a remittance-rich – and therefore relatively autonomous – citizenry and a poor state, to a poor and relatively economically dependent citizenry and an oil-rich state.[5] This shift was reflected in the renegotiation of the political settlement, favouring the regime rather than Yemen's social forces.

Like the rest of the Arab World, therefore, the rules of Yemen's political game are still being negotiated, and this complex and fluid process is occurring within a fundamentally different international context to the one in which Western states were forged. The relatively effective political settlements found in Western states, which were forged over centuries, were usually the result of protracted violent conflict.[6] Times have changed, and international laws and norms surrounding belligerency are far less permissive than they were in the early twentieth century. While this means that weak states have greater protection available to them from predatory neighbours, it also enables the survival of states and institutions that are not necessarily well adapted to their environment. The sovereignty – and sometimes territorial and fiscal integrity – of weak states is guaranteed to a significant degree by external sources, which can undermine the need for robust internal sources, such as popular legitimacy, or a productive economy.[7] Furthermore, in the post-colonial era, the reduced need for states to build and finance armies as a means of survival against external attack has had the knock-on effect of sometimes reducing survival-based incentives for states to build their tax-gathering and bureaucratic capabilities to support an an effective military. A second important difference between the international environment that shaped Western states and the one that is now shaping post-colonial Middle Eastern states is that many in the latter category can trade petrodollars (or strategic rents) for Western arms, which artificially increases the ability of the rulers to coerce the ruled.[8] At the turn of the century, the Middle East already spent more of its GDP per capita on defence than any other region. Between 1999 and 2008, that spending increased by another 34%.[9]

With this difference in mind, it is unrealistic to insist, as Western diplomats and leaders have done following the removal of Mubarak, that transitions from dictatorships to fledgling democracies must be orderly. This is particularly unrealistic given that the international weapons trade, the international reliance on oil and the Western tendency to view the region through a lens of counter-terrorism objectives have all helped to sustain these regimes, but cannot realistically be altered by those who take to the street in protest. Moving beyond the prevailing patterns of leadership in the Middle East will almost certainly be disruptive, if it is achievable. Real change is seldom orderly; in fact it tends to be messy, ad hoc and uncertain. Narrating these events, as Western policymakers are, with the overriding expectation of stability and orderliness risks making anything less than this high benchmark appear to be a failure – which it may not be. Middle Eastern states – including Yemen – are at a critical juncture in a complex transitional phase, with no clearly defined end-state. Western states can nonetheless insist that these regimes cease their brutal crackdowns on peaceful civilian protest, using diplomatic muscle and the threat of withdrawing financial support.

Why was nothing being done?

For several years, Yemen has been widely described by both foreign and local observers as experiencing escalating and multiple threats to its viability.[10] There have been many clear warning signs that a serious political crisis was building, so why were Yemen's elites unwilling and/or unable to take effective action against these threats? Why were they so ineffective at addressing serious threats to the viability of the state and to the wellbeing of its citizens? Was this failure primarily attributable to individual leaders – that is, to human agency – or were the leaders and elites constrained by structural factors beyond their control? Some theories of economic development suggest that an obvious threat, danger or opportunity facing the political leadership can create strong incentives for them to act in a manner that produces national economic development,[11] but to date this has not occurred in Yemen. This may be because the leadership did not consider the threats severe enough to warrant far-reaching reforms, or because they felt assured that financial aid from neighbours and Western powers could keep the problem under control. However, if there was the perception that a serious threat did exist, how can we explain the most significant barriers to effective action?

Approach

The data that forms the basis of this study was collected in mid-2010[12] for the Developmental Leadership Program[13] – before the crisis had found the catalyst that presented itself in early 2011. A cross-section of technocrats in government and the formal political party elite were questioned about the level of threat facing the country, the actions that they believed were required to respond adequately to the crisis and the obstacles that they faced in attempting to implement those solutions.

The sample of 64 respondents was divided into two approximately equal groups of 35 from the General People's Congress (GPC), or ruling party, and 29 from the Joint Meeting Parties (JMP), a relatively loose coalition of opposition parties. The aim was to survey as wide a group as possible among those within the JMP and GPC that are at least somewhat developmentally inclined. The research team considered the term 'developmentally inclined' to consist of three broad benchmarks: at the lower end of the spectrum are those who believe that the rule of law and the guarantee of equal citizenship are necessary functions of the state. We estimated this view is genuinely held by about 70% of the total bureaucratic and party elite. The next benchmark refers to those who believe that anti-corruption legislation should be strengthened, that strong state institutions are necessary, and that there should be relatively equal opportunity of access to government employment. We estimated that this view is genuinely held by about half of the total bureaucratic and party elite. Finally, we considered the third benchmark to be those who might be termed liberals, insofar as they believe there should be equal opportunities for women and greater government transparency. Around 25% of the total bureaucratic and political party elite fall into this category. Under these guidelines, close to 95% of those surveyed for this study are at least somewhat developmentally inclined.[14]

Through the responses to the survey and other primary and secondary source material, a picture begins to emerge of the regime's apparent perceptions of the level of threat posed to its ability to maintain power.[15] Institutions, policies and the seeming malignancy of the rent-based patronage system are clear to see; but what is less visible is the actors' perceptions of the political context in which they operate, their ability to shape that context and the collective action problems they face in so doing. It is only by looking at these factors together that external actors might apply incentives and disincentives more effectively in developing states and better understand the impacts and limitations of their own actions. By looking at the beliefs that the Yemeni power elite held about its environment and the strategies devised on this basis, it may be possible to discern the structural and agential barriers to developmental change within Yemen's political context.[16] The term agential is used here to refer to the ability of individuals to make choices or to innovate within the structural and institutional circumstances in which they operate. Having a better map of the structural and agential barriers to political change is valuable because the relationship between these two variables has a fundamental impact on the ability to target solutions: it is pointless, for example, to prescribe structural solutions to problems that are caused by agential or political processes, just as it is pointless to incentivise a leadership to act differently if the barriers to change are structural.

The influence of perception and agency in processes of development is analysed by Robert Bates in his book *When Things Fell Apart: State Failure in Late-Century Africa*.[17] He argues that political order results when two conditions occur simultaneously. The first condition is that the political leadership – which he refers to collectively as 'specialists in violence' – perceives that its interests are better served by employing coercive capacity to protect society's ability to create wealth than it is by preying upon that wealth. The second condition is that individuals in society collectively perceive that their interests are better served by trusting the specialists in violence to provide their security, thus allowing them to 'choose to set weapons aside and to devote their time to the production of wealth and to the enjoyment of leisure'.[18] Drawing on Charles Tilly's famous aphorism that states make wars and wars make states,[19] Bates argues elsewhere that a state's political leadership requires the capital and industry that merchants and investors can provide if it is to successfully coerce and wage war, while merchants and investors require the protection of private property that those with the means to coerce can provide.[20] He argues that when both the political and the economic elite perceive that their ability to survive rests upon their ability to cooperate, then political order and prosperity is more likely to prevail.[21]

Bates also argues that in the international system that emerged after the Second World War, the safeguards to sovereignty moved beyond the borders of the state and meant that 'political elites did not tend to treat economic policy as a matter of political survival'.[22] The effect of the external guarantees of sovereignty was that survival incentives were skewed and political elites could bargain with external actors for the economic resources necessary for their survival instead of with those in society who are capable of creating national wealth. In the absence of a survival incentive for pursuing developmental outcomes, development has become as much a matter for international negotiation as it is a matter for domestic negotiation.[23] In the prevailing international system, states are not necessarily compelled to nurture their local economies because income can be negotiated from external sources through international transfers.[24]

These insights are particularly relevant to understanding the Yemeni regime's perceived incentives to bargain with the international community for its political legitimacy and economic survival, as viewed against its perceived incentives to bargain with society for these same goods. Until the forced resignation of Egyptian President Mubarak in February 2011 powerfully illustrated Arab citizens' capacity for effective resistance, Yemen's power elite appeared to believe that the various crises did not seriously threaten their ability to maintain power. The key proviso to this was that they believed they could maintain access to sufficient rentier income from neighbours and, less significantly, from Western donors, and that there were no clear political alternatives to their rule. The uprisings in Tunisia and Egypt caught them entirely off guard. The threat that Yemen poses to regional and international security has also helped to underwrite the regime's ability to extract funds and thus maintain power. External actors have, therefore, affected the regime's agential behaviour by adjusting the structural circumstances in which it operates. The question for Western donors is whether they can affect these circumstances in a way that creates incentives for developmentally progressive behaviour.

The level of agreement that was expressed across party lines in the survey results about the seriousness of the threats facing the country was striking. Without exception, every participant believed that Yemen was facing 'serious problems', although there was some variation in whether it was felt that the problems are 'serious but temporary' or 'insurmountable and permanent'. Nearly four-fifths (79%) of participants believed that the latter category described at least one of the problems that they mentioned. It was commonly stated by participants that they could not understand why the Yemeni leadership (almost always a byword for Yemeni President Ali Abdullah Saleh) had not enacted some of the more obvious and achievable measures to reduce the pervasive instability. The prevalence of this view among participants was indicative of the widespread belief that President Saleh was relatively unconstrained by his circumstances. His individual agency was seen as the fundamental driver of Yemen's problems, and it was therefore widely held by the formal political and technocratic elite that he could decisively alter the country's political and economic trajectory if that were his decision.

What follows is an examination of the veracity of this assumption and of the structural and political context in which the president and his powerful, though opaque, inner circle operated for more than 32 years. The term 'elites' refers to the small and fluid group of individuals that occupy 'the most powerful positions'[25] in a country's political system. As is discussed below, the Yemeni elite is comprised of tribal sheiks, military leaders, religious leaders, political party elites, technocrats and, to a lesser degree, traditional merchants. These elites are responsible for setting and pursuing the national agenda, though this is not necessarily to imply that the interests of the elite are aligned with the interests of the average citizen. Broadly speaking, Yemen's political elites are not developmentally inclined, particularly as one moves up the regime's hierarchy, although there are some exceptions to this.

Key players

Before discussing the context of this study further, it is necessary to briefly introduce the key players, although this will be done in far greater detail later in Chapters 5 and 6. This study examines four main groups of actors: the JMP, GPC, the regime and the regime's 'inner circle'.

The JMP, a coalition of six opposition parties, is dominated by its strongest and most popular member, the Islamist Islah Party, which currently holds 46 of the 301 seats in the parliament that was elected in 2003. The next most important party in the coalition is the Yemeni Socialist Party (YSP), which was the former ruling party of the south Yemeni state (the People's Democratic Republic of Yemen), and holds seven seats in parliament. The Nasserite Party holds three seats, and has a small base of popular support, while the Ba'ath Party holds one seat. The other members of the coalition, Hizb al-Haqq and the Union of Popular Forces (UPF), do not have any seats in parliament and are not considered to be electorally significant, although al-Haqq has gained some popularity in the past few years. The importance of these smaller parties in the JMP coalition is largely in displaying to the regime that all of Yemen's opposition parties are united under one umbrella; there is low ideological and policy consensus between the member parties.

The GPC is Yemen's ruling party, and dominates the country's formal political party environment. Its key function and purpose is to extend patronage to politically and socially relevant elites and to provide the formal institutional base of support for President Saleh. The GPC is not an ideological party: like the JMP, it incorporates a diverse group of elites under a broad umbrella. Unlike the JMP, however, membership in the GPC brings benefits for ordinary citizens, some of whom are able to obtain employment or other tangible benefits. Generally speaking, membership in the JMP does not bring benefits to ordinary citizens.

Elites within the political party system are *not* the most powerful actors in the Yemeni system and most, but not all, are not considered members of the regime. Most, however, can be considered part of the 'establishment' that maintains the political system. The party elite was chosen for this study for several reasons, the most important of which was the desire to explain the failure of the JMP to galvanise wider support for its demands for political and economic reform, despite widespread discontent with the status quo. The second reason was the impossibility of obtaining candid access to a *representative* selection of the power elite who would be willing to speak on the record.

The 'regime' refers to the network of elites (now predominantly tribal and military personalities) whose interests are considered on an adhoc and fluid basis by the president and his inner circle in political decisions. Being a member of the GPC does not imply a person's membership in the regime and neither does a person's membership in the regime necessarily indicate that they are members of the GPC, although there is greater correlation on the latter point. There are several – non-mutually exclusive and fluid – pillars of political power in Yemen, including the tribal elite, the religious elite and the military elite.[26] The more politically significant actors within these groups are, the more deeply embedded they are in the regime's patronage networks.

The regime's 'inner circle' refers to a narrow and highly opaque group of approximately 50 people that surround President Ali Abdullah Saleh, drawn from his family and tribe – the Sanhan. The members of this group who serve as military commanders are well known to the Yemeni public but the rest are covered in a shroud of secrecy. It is the inner machinations of this inner circle that has been most crucial to the developmental trajectory of the Yemeni state. As is discussed below, it is difficult to gather verifiable data about this group. Political power is concentrated in the president and his inner circle, and in many ways the regime is best understood in dynastic terms. The close kin, extended family and followers have been the most important players in the game throughout his rule.

CHAPTER ONE

The nature of the threat

After years of unrealised promises to implement major reforms to prevent an economic collapse and reduce political violence, the Yemeni state is grappling with severe challenges on several fronts simultaneously. It is facing a series of deepening economic and political challenges, including declining oil and water reserves, budget shortfalls, civil conflict, a burgeoning civil protest movement, foreign military intervention, pervasive poverty and an increasingly aggressive militant jihadi movement. Whoever follows President Ali Abdullah Saleh will have to grapple with the potentially crippling fact that the country is running out of the resources it requires to feed itself. This section will outline the nature, and the local perceptions, of those challenges.

Security threats

The scale of the civil protest movement that was sparked by the forced resignation of the Egyptian president in February 2011 is unprecedented in Yemen. Young protesters from diverse parts of the country have merged the various strains of political discontent that have been evident for years, adopting the simple refrain that President Saleh must leave office. However, even prior to the protest, Yemeni citizens were already regularly challenging the legitimacy of the regime and there had been a visible retraction of state power in the periphery on the basis of these various challenges. By 2010, the state could not reliably access significant parts of seven of its 21 governorates: Abyan, Shabwa, al-Dhala'e, Marib, al-Jawf, Sa'da and Lahj. It is important to note, however, that expectation of full territorial control only existed after unification and that President Saleh has successfully maintained power throughout his career without ever really holding such expectations.

The 'Southern Movement' is arguably the most serious internal threat facing the integrity of the Yemeni state, although it receives less international attention than the other security threats because its focus is solely domestic.[1] Known simply as *al-Harak* (the movement) within Yemen, it refers to a number of loosely affiliated organisations and activists in the southern governorates who are protesting against the perceived injustices of the northern-based regime.[2] Southerners have long charged that northern elites have built their survival on the extraction of the south's natural resources, while entrenching a system that excludes southerners from government employment and other benefits. They argue that they have been stripped of their once-robust system of law and order (*nizam*) and have been subsumed by the chaotic and personalised rule (*fawda*) of the north.

In 2007 that discontent found a more formal voice, and by 2008 some had begun to openly call for secession at protests, and to raise the flag of the former southern state throughout the south. The early protests were against a set of specific grievances, particularly the forced retirement and insufficient pensions of southern military officers, but they quickly spread into a much wider phenomenon, even moving into the governorates of Ta'izz and Ibb, where they involved much broader issues of regime legitimacy. Despite the threat posed, the regime made no serious moves to deal with the grievances being expressed. Instead, it added fuel to the fire by continuing to illegally appropriate southern land.

As with most political issues in Yemen, there is heavy speculation domestically that the hand of Saudi Arabia can be seen behind the southern secessionist movement. While this has not been possible to prove, it is worthy of mention because of the prevalence of this view within Yemeni political circles.[3]

The insurgency that is being led by the al-Houthi family in the northern governorate of Sa'da also remains incendiary despite repeated attempts to finalise a ceasefire between the government and the insurgents.[4] The conflict has displaced around 265,000 people since it began in 2004 and resulted in direct military intervention from Saudi Arabia in late 2009. The involvement of Saudi Arabia is partly a result of the fact that the conflict is being conducted so close to its border, and the Kingdom's belief that the al-Houthis may be supported by Iran – a belief that the Yemeni government has done much to perpetuate.[5] By the end of 2010, the al-Houthis had gained control of the majority of the governorates of Sa'da and al-Jawf (in 12 of the 14 districts) and they had strong influence in the entire governorate of Hajja but no military control. They also controlled two districts in 'Amraan and two districts in Sana'a.

The regime charges that the al-Houthi family and their supporters, the Believing Youth (*Shabaab al-Mu'mineen*), have called for the reestablishment of the Zaydi imamate that governed northern Yemen for over 1,000 years (with brief interruptions) until 1962. As a family of sayyids – that is, those who claim descent from the Prophet Mohammed through his daughter Fatima and her husband Ali – members of the al-Houthi family would theoretically be eligible to claim the title of imam for themselves. Revival of the imamate is an idea which is rejected by Yemen's Sunni majority and many Zaydi tribespeople, and which stands in contradiction to the goal of the 1962 revolution to weaken the age-old power of the sayyids over other Zaydis who are not members of the ascriptive religious elite. As a Zaydi tribesman who is not a sayyid, President Saleh embodied that goal.[6]

However, what began as a relatively localised conflict in Sa'da has since expanded well beyond the area, involving tribal groups and foreign actors, for reasons that are at least partially related to internal rivalries within the regime's inner circle. These are discussed in greater detail in Chapter Five.

Al-Qaeda in the Arabian Peninsula (AQAP) has become increasingly aggressive and has stepped up its attacks against government personnel to an unprecedented level. Even before the death of Osama bin Laden in a US raid in March 2011, the group was seen by the US administration (and many in other Western governments and media outlets) to be 'perhaps the most dangerous of all the franchises of al-Qaeda right now'.[7] The real and perceived international threat posed by AQAP has served to sharpen Western concerns that the group may capitalise on the instability in Yemen to consolidate a base from which to target Western states.

AQAP has created an astute narrative surrounding the widely perceived injustices perpetrated by the regime. For example, an article in the tenth edition of Sada al-Malahim argued that 'The inhabitants of [the oil rich areas, Marib, Shabwa and Hadramaut] are paying for their own oppression' with the oil wealth misappropriated by their government.[8] This statement represented an important shift in the way that oil is usually discussed in al-Qaeda propaganda; the argument was not about the West greedily obtaining oil at any cost, but rather about local communities not receiving what was rightfully theirs because the government was corrupt and unjust. This built on a critique that was made in *Sada al-Malahim* two issues earlier, that:

> The people of Yemen are suffering from the decline of living standards, the rise of costs, and the discriminatory practices with which the government deals with them in employment, the distribution of wealth and its looting, the misappropriation of lands, and the absence of someone to defend their rights.[9]

With an increasingly under-nourished population and a rise in political dissent throughout significant parts of the country, AQAP picked up on the prevalent perception that the system is not working. There are not enough domestic resources for the oil-based patronage system to endure, and the regime has expended little effort on creating economic alternatives to oil. If AQAP's narrative can continue to link the suffering of ordinary Yemenis to the injustice of the regime and the complicity of the West, it is likely to continue to find space within which to operate. In this endeavour AQAP is probably assisted by comments by the US administration that suggest the burgeoning civil protest movement for a more inclusive political system are contrary to American interests. Speaking in the days following the 18 March massacre, for example, US Defense Secretary Robert Gates said: 'Instability and diversion of attention from [al-Qaeda] are my primary source of concern [in Yemen].'[10] US Ambassador to Yemen Gerald Feierstein reiterated this al-Qaeda-centric stance: 'We believe that the uncertainty and the instability is helpful to al-Qaeda.'[11] Perhaps more helpful to AQAP, however, is the perception within Yemen that the United States government would rather see the endurance of the Yemeni regime than risk the possibility of a new political order.

Socio-economic threats

Like much of the Middle East, the population of Yemen has a large youth bulge. Over 75% of Yemen's population is under the age of 25,[12] in a country where unofficial estimates usually place unemployment at around 40%. Yemen also now has one of the most food-insecure populations in the world, with 42% of children being malnourished. In a 2010 study on food security, the World Food Programme (WFP) reported that: 'about 6.8m Yemenis (31.5%) are food-insecure and, within this group, 2.5m people (11.8%) were found to be severely food-insecure'.[13] As food prices reached all-time highs in early 2011,[14] these percentages looked certain to climb.

As the level of food security for ordinary Yemenis declines, popular discontent about this issue is plainly apparent and although the author is not aware of any scientific studies to determine the extent of this discontent, one indicative study warrants mention. In 2008, the Yemen Polling Center (YPC) conducted a series of training sessions that aimed to teach political-party members how to conduct basic public-opinion surveys. To illustrate the methodology of scientific polling, the YPC put a sample poll into the field asking participants several questions about their perceptions of the country's situation. The results illustrated popular perceptions of the overall negative direction of travel in Yemen.

The poll sampled views from 224 participants from six governorates, only 6.7% of whom reported being illiterate (despite national levels being around 50%). This low level of illiteracy highlights that the poll must be treated as indicative only, and it cannot be considered truly random because it favoured participants from wealthier governorates and with higher than average levels of education. Further, women constituted only 10.7% of participants. However, the overall picture presented by the poll was compelling, particularly considering that the participants were in positions of relative advantage. In response to the question 'how would you describe your living condition in the last 12 months?', 16% said that it had improved, while 66.5% said it had become worse and 16.5% noticed no difference. However, participants strongly perceived a decline in other people's situations. When asked how they would describe Yemenis' living situation in general, 84.4% thought the situation had become worse, while less than 5% believed that it had improved, and less than 9% saw no difference. Finally, the poll suggested that most people (54.9%) expect this trend to worsen over the next five years, while only 17.4% thought it would improve. However, what is more revealing was that the Yemeni government was so concerned by the poll that pressure was successfully applied for it not to be released publicly.

The most serious structural threats facing Yemen are the decline of its two most important natural resources: water and oil. Yemen is one of the most water-scarce countries in the world and it is believed that the capital city of Sana'a could run out of fresh water within 15 years.[15] Diminishing supplies are contributing to land disputes as people try to gain or maintain access to groundwater. However, part of the problem derives from the fact that water is an undervalued commodity. Yemen's groundwater is extracted using diesel-generated pumps and, for political reasons that are discussed later, diesel has been heavily subsidised by the Saleh regime. The subsidy on diesel is directly connected to the unsustainable extraction of groundwater.

Oil production has fallen faster than the government had anticipated and there is no other source of income likely to replace it before oil revenues drop to, or below, subsistence level.[16] The Yemeni economy is in serious trouble: the budget deficit was estimated to be 9.3% of GDP for 2010[17] and crude oil (the country's main export) production fell by around 4% in the first quarter of 2010, compared with the same period in 2009.[18] In 2010, for example, the government's operating costs were expected to exceed its income by around 30%,[19] and by early 2011 the situation had become critical as President Saleh continued to induce supporters with cash incentives. Since 2008, the regime has had less money to distribute through its networks each year. Oil revenue dropped by around 40% in 2009, further hamstringing the government's already strained budget. The Economist Intelligence Unit (EIU) estimated even before the 2011 uprisings that Yemen's real GDP growth for 2011–2012 would drop to an average of less than 3%, which is less than the country's annual population growth and 'insufficient to prevent increasing economic hardship'.[20] The drop in oil revenues is not being recouped through gas exports, greater foreign investment or labour remittances, for reasons that are partly political and are discussed later. While the regime repeatedly claimed that the revenue from gas exports would largely replace the income from oil exports, in May 2010 it admitted that the income from gas in 2010 was less than a quarter of what had it had hoped.[21] Despite these declines, almost nothing of substance has been done to plan for a post-rentier economy.

In June 2010, President Saleh announced that Yemen had actually already become a net oil importer.[22] If true, this would have meant that Yemen's political economy, so heavily reliant on the centralised dispersal of oil rents, could no longer have continued to operate in the manner that it had since oil exports began. However, it appears that President Saleh was intentionally understating the country's oil exports in an attempt to convince donors to approve direct budget subsidies instead of the more conditional assistance that was then on the table. Negotiations with the IMF had collapsed for this reason, with the Yemeni government insisting that the IMF offer a direct budget subsidy of $1.5bn per year, while the IMF was offering $350m over three years in balance-of-payment support.

Just two months after the president's startling announcement, Yemen's oil minister, Amir al-Aidaroos, reported triumphantly that the country's oil revenues had risen dramatically. One state-owned news agency reported that Yemen's share of oil revenues for January to May totalled $1.132bn, 'sharply higher than the $483.24m for the same period of 2009'.[23] The blatantly contradictory statements of the president and the minister – by no means unusual in the Yemeni context – illustrate that even the country's most important economic data can be open to interpretation or intentional obfuscation. This level of opacity means that facts and counter-facts are volleyed back and forth, often with few reliably authentic reference points. Even those tasked with verifying Yemen's data for international lending institutions report their lack of confidence in Yemen's indicators. In a meeting with three senior economists from the Yemen World Bank office and the Headquarters of the World Bank in March 2010, it was acknowledged that even their economic forecasts necessarily involve a level of guesswork because they must accept government statistics at face value. This level of uncertainty makes it very difficult for Yemen's technocrats and donors alike to confidently predict Yemen's future indicators with any precision. The result is that the belief in Yemen's dangerous volatility is reinforced.

Political threats: Saleh's exclusionary model

Despite its rapid depletion, Yemen's power elite has not endeavoured to either conserve or protect the country's oil reserves.[24] Diesel smuggling is a perennial problem in Yemen.

An unpublished study by the author and Abdul-Ghani al-Iryani in 2008 illustrated the impact of the smuggling on the country's capacity to remain economically viable. Diesel is the most heavily subsidised item in Yemen, and the 2008 study found that at least 50% of the public money allocated to the diesel subsidy (in 2008, around $3.5bn, or 12% of GDP[25]) was either smuggled or transferred on paper by the regime's elite, who resold it at the international price – at tremendous profit. Diesel smuggling has increased considerably in the past decade, which can be seen in the large increases in diesel imports relative to domestic consumption. The figures illustrate this increase starkly: in 2000 Yemen imported 508,989 tonnes of diesel; by 2006, this had more than tripled to 1.796m tonnes, before dropping slightly to 1.681m tonnes in 2007. A cursory glance at Yemen's economic growth statistics shows that this type of increase is vastly incommensurate with economic growth in that same period. The discrepancy cannot be explained by increases to electricity generation, because electricity is generated by imported fuel oil, the import rate of which has not matched diesel.[26]

In January 2008, an officially sanctioned exposé in *al-Shaari'a* (a local newspaper funded by the Office of the President) confirmed long-standing popular speculation over the nature and cost of the smuggling:

> Official estimates of the cost of diesel and LPG [liquid petroleum gas] smuggling to the country [in 2007] is 180 billion riyals [$900m] ... The profits of smugglers are horrendous; the cost is heavy to the nation and to the president personally, for in addition to his responsibility to the public by merit of his office he is directly hurt by smuggling since his name is used as a cover, and the names of many of the pillars of his state are cited as the patrons of this drain to the country.[27]

This article was perhaps a shot across the bow, as President Saleh attempted to gauge the reaction within his inner circle to reducing some of the more blatant corruption. If it was, no further action was taken – one might guess because of a negative reaction within his inner circle.

Furthermore, the amount of revenue that is lost to diesel smuggling by the power elite does not account for other forms of economic loss and environmental degradation associated with the diesel and petroleum subsidies. This is most apparent in the way that the subsidy denies the state revenue and encourages widespread overuse by artificially inducing people to unsustainably pump groundwater using diesel-generated pumps. The smuggling and the unsustainability of the subsidy are two different issues. A developmentally inclined and politically powerful elite could theoretically elect to stop the smuggling; however, the removal of the diesel subsidy would also be politically difficult. Yemen's petroleum subsidies are popularly, though erroneously, believed by ordinary Yemenis to be a pro-poor initiative. As the figures above clearly illustrate, this is incorrect because the subsidies are a mechanism for transferring the national budget to the power elite. A well-crafted public education campaign, which included the details of the smuggling, would be required to overcome the likely discontent that this necessary move would bring. This is politically charged because it would necessarily expose the level of corruption inherent within the inner circle. Local observers estimate, for example, that one particular member of the regime's inner circle made $155m from diesel smuggling in 2006, and that this man's profit was not unusual.[28] The World Bank's second Quarterly Report for Yemen for 2010 shows that the amount spent on subsidies has changed little between 2009 and 2010 (it increased from 8.2 % to 8.7 % of GDP) despite acute diesel shortages on the Yemeni street.[29]

The above illustrates that a large portion of Yemen's population faces conditions of high vulnerability. But vulnerability experienced at the lower levels of society does not necessarily create comparable vulnerability for regime's power elite, unless it is combined with other environmental changes. In one analysis, Richard Doner, Bryan Ritchie and Dan Slater argue that for a regime to experience an 'extraordinarily constrained political environment' there must be three simultaneous conditions: the credible threat of mass unrest resulting from the deterioration of living standards; an increased need for military equipment and foreign exchange; and serious budget constraints resulting from insufficient exploitable sources of revenue.[30] While the overwhelming majority of elites within the political party system said they believed the threat facing the country required urgent action, the regime's inner circle did not. This difference in perception begins to explain why the president and his inner circle approached Yemen's challenges with such apparent nonchalance despite the many warning signs.

CHAPTER TWO

The regime, the West and the language of reform

Western perceptions of Yemen tend to be filtered through local elites, the most accessible and persuasive of which maintain their credibility on the basis of speaking fluent English and perpetuating the external belief in Yemen's inordinate complexity and danger. This view is better understood against the backdrop of Yemen's power structures and the means by which they have endured. Among the most significant features of these are the international aspect of Yemen's political viability, the securitisation of the foreign assistance offered to Yemen and the sources of President Saleh's domestic legitimacy.

As is true in many developing polities, the most notable feature of Yemen's formal institutions is their relative lack of salience compared to the informal institutions. Neither power nor wealth is generated or transmitted predominantly through the state's formal institutions. The power of Yemen's formal state organisations is far less than it appears on paper, and the institutions themselves are broadly subservient to the interests of the regime, particularly President Saleh. The same can be said for the constitution, which articulates the formal rules of Yemen's political game but is largely ignored in daily political affairs. However, while they are overshadowed, Yemen's formal institutions are not entirely irrelevant and some, such as the parliament and certain local councils, are sufficiently representative of their constituencies to act as a barometer of popular sentiment on at least a small number of issues. However, the final decision about how to respond to popular concerns raised through these organisations remains the purview of a narrow group. Yemen's formal organisations, particularly the military and the ruling party, the GPC, are also important to the regime's ability to reproduce its rule throughout the country. The formal organisations that possess even a modicum of popular representation are also crucial to the regime's ability to interact with Western government and donor agencies and could, conceivably, form the foundation of a more empowered formal sector in the post-Saleh era.

The formal political settlement

The Republic of Yemen was created on 22 May 1990, under the unity agreement between North Yemen, then led by Ali Abdullah Saleh, and his counterpart from South Yemen, Ali Salim al-Beidh. The haste with which unification was achieved proved a key determinant of how Yemen's formal institutions were forged, and gives important clues regarding the gap between the formal organisations and the informal political processes that drive actors' behaviour.

Throughout the 1970s and 80s, there was a series of unsuccessful attempts to unify the two states, so when the leaders agreed again in May 1988 to 'revive the unified political organisation as stipulated in Article Nine of the Tripoli Statement' (an agreement to unify north and south Yemen made 1972), many observers believed that this was likely to be another false start.[1] However, as popular anticipation built, so too did pressure on the two leaders to conclude a binding agreement.

That agreement was made in November 1989 at a summit in the southern capital of Aden. Formal unification took place just six months later, although it was originally intended that there would be a full year dedicated to the transition.[2]

The new Yemeni constitution, ratified in 1991, laid the formal foundation for a democratic state. Universal suffrage was granted to citizens over the age of 18, with the promise of regular elections, and considerable freedom of expression and political association. The neighbouring regime of Saudi Arabia denounced the notion of elections, and particularly the inclusion of women in the process, as 'un-Islamic'.[3] To many other observers, however, the new Yemeni constitution was a remarkably liberal document and there was considerable optimism that it signalled the growth of the 'third wave' of democratisation in the historically illiberal Middle East.[4] The idea that Yemen is a transitional democracy remained an important part of the Yemeni government's credibility with Western donors, despite the fact that the liberalism outlined in the first constitution was substantially eroded in subsequent constitutional amendments in 1994 and 2001. This point will be revisited shortly with regard to the regime's ongoing reform agendas, and the role of Western donors within that process.

A question that continues to puzzle observers is why the new government opted to ratify a constitution that was such an apparent political outlier in the region. One possible answer is that Yemen has a strong consultative tradition, albeit among the country's elites, and that traditional tribal authority – itself founded on a relatively egalitarian basis – is consensus-driven. A sheikh is, at least ideally, a representative of his community to outsiders, not a law unto himself. It is not uncommon to hear Yemenis argue on this basis that these traditions render Yemen more likely than some other Arab states to weave these local political norms into a formal democratic system. It is also widely argued that because Yemen's tribes are so well armed, the regime believed that it needed to establish organisations that were capable of bargaining with a diverse array of local leaders, many of whom aspired to a considerable level of autonomy from the state. Others have argued, however, that the notion of a democratic transition was cynically intended to attract Western donor aid.[5] The fact that Yemen's requests for foreign aid are often qualified with a reminder that such assistance would 'ensure the continuation of democracy'[6] lends some credence to the latter claim.

However, another important and often-overlooked factor was the speed with which unification was achieved. Being drafted in haste, the 1991 constitution was based on an existing document that had been principally drafted in the 1970s by two technocratic constitutional scholars, Isma'il al-Wazeer and Hussein al-Hubbeishi.[7] The earlier document was drafted after the Tripoli Statement. The 1972 pledge to unify the two nations was not considered to be sincere by either side and consequently it was not believed that the resulting constitution would be implemented. The drafters were thus given considerable latitude to craft a document, the outcome of which was one that adhered more to international constitutional norms and best practices than it did to Yemen's political realities.[8] Being drafted on this basis, the 1991 constitution did not outline the de facto rules of Yemen's political game. In a further indication of the document's detachment from local realities, it was amended in 1994 after the civil war and again in 2001, with each amendment rolling back the promises contained in the initial document, and extending the formal power of the executive.

Prior to unification, the leaderships on both sides of the border considered informal politics to be the main theatre of political competition, and neither state was notably limited by the dictates of their constitutions. In the South, for example, the national formula (*al-mu'adalah al-watania*) was an informal understanding that all major social and regional groups should be represented at all levels of government. Every time the 'formula' was challenged – in 1969, 1978 and 1986 – there was serious armed violence that resulted in a shift of political power between the elites from one regional group to the other.[9]

The language of reform

President Saleh has long adopted the language of developmental reform. In an initiative announced on 22 May 2010, for example, he called for a serious and 'responsible national dialogue … among the full political spectrum and all of the sons of the homeland in the country and abroad'. In a cabinet meeting held just days after the announcement, he vowed 'to go on with economic and administrative reforms, cut down on public expenditure, re-evaluate the subsidies on petroleum products, raise civil service and military salaries, and expand the social welfare network, stop diesel smuggling, [and] review the natural LNG contracts'. He also reaffirmed his intention to expand local administration and renewed his 'call for serious and responsible dialogue' with national political forces based on his 22 May initiative, saying that 'dialogue is the optimal method for dealing with country's problems'.[10] His actions failed to match his rhetoric on each of these points; each issue had been a standard part of his public rhetoric for several years. Furthermore, Saleh proposed a package of constitutional amendments in early January 2011, in which the two-term limit for a president was removed. This left little doubt that his intention was – at least until events in Tunisia and Egypt articulated serious cautionary tales – to further centralise political power.

As the rest of this chapter will demonstrate, while there has been a clear incentive for President Saleh to use developmental language, there was also a clear threat to him and his inner circle if he went so far as to implement developmental policies. Another factor keeping development off the agenda in the years following the invasion of Iraq is counter-terrorism. Reform and counter-terrorism objectives became increasingly entangled during this time. In November 2005, President Saleh visited the United States and was reportedly expecting a warm reception for the demonstrable progress that his regime had made against al-Qaeda in Yemen.[11] By late 2005, al-Qaeda affiliates in Yemen had been largely defeated, and its members either killed or imprisoned. President Saleh felt, with some justification, that he had turned around a potentially calamitous issue for the US and deserved credit for what had been achieved. Instead of accolades for progress on security objectives, however, President Saleh was admonished for the rising levels of corruption in all levels of the Yemeni government. President Saleh was told by the CEO of the Millennium Challenge Corporation (MCC), John J. Danilovich, that Yemen was no longer eligible to take part in the threshold programme due to his government's worsening performance in the 'control of corruption' category.[12]

After his meeting with the MCC, President Saleh met with Secretary of State Condoleezza Rice, who also 'rapped him over the knuckles' for failing to deliver on his previous promises to implement necessary political and economic reforms.[13] She told him that if he did not begin to instigate credible reforms, the US would not view him as a legitimate candidate in the 2006 presidential elections. The following day, the World Bank followed suit and reduced its upcoming three-year loan package by 34% (from $420 million to $280m), also citing Yemen's lack of transparency and good governance.[14] President Saleh was stunned at the very public rebuke, and promptly fired his economic advisers.[15] Shortly after his return to Yemen he sponsored a new National Reform Agenda by the Ministry of International Planning and Cooperation (MOPIC) to improve 'Yemen's investment climate and strengthen … democratic institutions'.[16] However, the message that was, certainly unintentionally, conveyed to President Saleh during his trip to the United States was that without the threat of al-Qaeda, Yemen could be subject to much more stringent conditions on its domestic politics.[17] Just months after this, in February 2006, 23 al-Qaeda suspects broke out from a maximum-security prison in such an audacious escape that it is widely understood to have been impossible without inside assistance. Some of those 23 men went on to establish al-Qaeda in the Arabian Peninsula (AQAP), putting Yemen's problem with militant jihadis was back on the international agenda.

Meanwhile, the National Reform Agenda (which President Saleh had announced shortly after the trip to the United States) was adopted as a pillar of the president's campaign in the September 2006 elections. The elections were deemed relatively free and fair by international observers and were followed in November by a conference at Lancaster House in London, in which Western and Gulf Cooperation Council donors pledged a total of $4.7 billion in aid to Yemen. By mid-2007, the Millennium Challenge Corporation was similarly encouraged, and determined that Yemen had made sufficient progress in anti-corruption measures to be re-admitted to the threshold programme. At the time Yemen's re-admission was seen as a considerable victory for reformers within the government, who had worked to lay the foundations for more robust anti-corruption legislation.

However, in October 2007 as the final preparations were being made to sign over the $20.6m in development aid that Yemen's reacceptance to the MCC brought, President Saleh decided to release Yemen's most-wanted al-Qaeda operative

– the architect of the USS *Cole* bombing, Jamal al-Badawi –
to house arrest.[18] He did this very publicly, on the basis that
Badawi had surrendered to the Yemeni authorities and promised to renounce violence. The timing of the release – the day
before the $20.6m was to be delivered to the Yemeni govern-
ment – makes it almost incomprehensible that President Saleh
was not underlining his autonomy from American money, and
possibly from the expectations of the technocrats in his government.[19] The United States was furious and instantly suspended
Yemen from the MCC programme again, this time for failing
to cooperate on counter-terrorism measures. Those in Yemen
who had worked towards reinstatement were angered by the
suspension and felt that the US had moved the goalposts in
a programme that was ostensibly unrelated to security objectives.[20] The reformers complained that the suspension only
handed ammunition to those that were already opposed to
reform. The message that was reinforced this time was that
where the US is concerned, political development comes a
poor second to cooperation against al-Qaeda. The inconsis-
tency with which Washington has pursued political reform
and security objectives in Yemen has undermined its ability to
argue that security and development are indivisible elements
of a coherent policy.

Some of the GPC's genuine reformers, including Jalal
Yacoub, then a deputy minister in MOPIC, decided to try to
convince donors to return to Yemen.[21] In 2008, Yacoub wrote
an article in the newspaper *Yemen Today*,[22] which argued that
the government needed to pursue ten reforms as priorities
in order to maintain Yemen's viability.[23] Despite Yacoub's
position in MOPIC, the plan was not developed as a minis-
terial initiative but instead appeared to be in competition
with the National Reform Agenda that was being championed through MOPIC. Yacoub's idea evolved into the 'Ten

Point Plan', which was also supported by two others in the Executive Committee (an informal group established in 2008 to drive reforms),[24] and has since attracted some Western interest.

In the words of one Western donor, the Ten Point Plan seemed at least partly a public relations initiative by reformers.[25] Western donor assistance was sought for the plan from 2008 but donors were uneasy about the unwillingness of the Executive Committee to approach the regime for funding, which raised questions over whether the plan really did have the support of President Saleh, as they were being assured. In August 2009, President Saleh officially endorsed the plan but donors and diplomats in Yemen reported remaining uncertain of his actual level of commitment.[26]

From the outset, there were questions over who would fund the initiative. Western donors argued that, if the Yemeni government wanted to demonstrate that it was serious about reform, it should fund at least one of the ten initiatives as an indication of that commitment. The Executive Committee openly considered the first of the ten points, a plan to reinvent the civil service by bringing in 100 highly skilled technocrats, through a comprehensive programme to attract talent into the civil service, to be the most fundamental.[27] These 'top 100' (later increased to 150) would be recruited on merit, offered attractive salaries and given wide latitude to improve the efficiency of the bureaucracy. As one Western donor said in November 2010:

> We told them that they could afford it; it would not have been very expensive. However, the concern was not that the Yemenis were asking for something that they could afford, it was a question of political commitment: why aren't they funding this themselves

when it *is* affordable? If [the Committee] can't even persuade President Saleh to fund this inexpensive initiative, what does it say about his commitment to the Ten Point Plan more broadly?[28]

Despite this, pressure increased on donors to fund the plan and again, assurances were offered that it was supported at the highest levels of the regime and, moreover, that there was now an insider who would ensure its passage through any informal obstacles. It was later revealed that this insider was President Saleh's son Ahmed Ali, although his identity was initially not known for certain by donors. The secrecy surrounding the group's patron led to the Executive Committee to be informally dubbed 'the Committee with No Name' by some donors.[29] The pressure for external funding became so intense that one Western donor noted:

> If we were to sign over any money for this plan, I would have to say to my government that that my Yemeni counterpart is a member of the president's family whom I cannot name, and whom my minister cannot meet. I understand that informal structures exist, and that they exist everywhere, but we cannot support such an opaque shadow state.[30]

This illustrates a serious tension for donors. They need to engage with their formal counterparts, such as MOPIC, but to be effective they also need to engage with the real power brokers in the shadow state. How donors reconcile these two is one of the most fundamental issues that they face, particularly when they are not willingly given direct access to the real decision-makers. At the same time, donors need to push much more consistently and assertively for this access.

Despite early reservations surrounding the Ten Point Plan, it has gained traction internationally. As another Western diplomat argued:

> They have used external support cleverly, particularly the Americans and the British. [US Secretary of State] Hillary Clinton specifically mentioned the Ten Point Plan, as did [former UK Foreign Secretary] David Miliband, and they [the Committee] talk about the way that the US and the British like the plan. I think this shows how dependent it is on external support.[31]

The Ten Point Plan (which over the course of 2010 shrank to five 'priorities')[32] argues that the reforms it suggests are part of an urgent rescue plan intended to quickly stabilise Yemen's economy. It offers technical solutions to Yemen's bureaucratic inefficiencies, but does not address the deeper political processes that either permit or prevent their implementation. The issue of elite corruption is strikingly absent, particularly with regard to the diesel smuggling that occurs within the upper echelons of the regime, at a cost of at least $1bn annually. The waste incurred through subsidising diesel is addressed as though it is only a management issue that can be fixed by trimming costs. For example, the plan argues that the country can save about $200m a year by reducing the amount of the subsidy. However, a saving of $200m each year equates to only about a fifth of the amount that members of the regime siphoned off that year through smuggling. At any rate, the issue of diesel smuggling, like the potentially awkward issue of land disputes, was ultimately excised from the five priorities in favour of politically neutral calls to discover more oil and help more Yemenis find work in the GCC countries.

The Executive Committee was openly proud that the plan was a more honest reflection of domestic realities than previous reform plans, particularly the National Reform Agenda (2006) – and that it did not emerge simply as a product of donor pressure. However, the National Reform Agenda put anti-corruption measures as it first priority,[33] while the Ten Point Plan did not address the matter directly at all. As one member of the Executive Committee noted in an interview in mid-2010: 'The solution to Yemen's problems is the "top 150". Unlike the other reform programs that are forced on us by outsiders we have the Ten Point Plan, which we developed ourselves.'[34] Despite its grand claims, the domestically produced plan preferred not to target the redline issue of the corruption that supported the inner circle.

The evolution of the Ten Point Plan illustrates that the regime is both pragmatic and rational, and is also very capable of responding astutely in its interests to Western signals about its desired behaviour. The Executive Committee hired the international management consulting firm McKinsey to refine the plan (and presumably pitch it towards a Western audience) at a cost of $9m.[35] A leaked copy of McKinsey's 58-page draft White Paper, 'The Yemen Rescue Plan', published in September 2010, revealed that the word 'corruption' appears only once, and even this is only in passing.[36] The crux of the argument is that the Yemeni government requires foreign assistance to build capacity:

> In order for Yemen to reverse this decline, the government will need to drive improvement in its execution capability ... Yemen will require significant support from its donors if it is to achieve the aspired levels of investment and job creation.

However, this suggests the hope that increased investment could occur without needing to touch the inner circle.

This pragmatic response to external pressure – which was also apparent in the events that followed President Saleh's visit to the United States in November 2005 – probably grants Western actors more leverage than they believe they have. The fact that the reform agenda is given such prominence in the president's rhetoric suggests that the issue of reform is about more than the possibility of attracting Western donor funding – the amount of which is quite insignificant when compared to what has been made available by Yemen's neighbours. In fact, it points to two of President Saleh's perceived vulnerabilities: his desire to maintain the constitutional legitimacy that separated him from his inner circle, and the belief that he had something to fear from the West – most likely the possibility of either criminal prosecution or of military invasion. President Saleh, therefore, had incentives to maintain the view among Western governments that he was willing to enact reforms but was structurally constrained by an inefficient bureaucracy. The Western plan to 'stabilise', which now forms the basis of donor engagement in Yemen, has taken this too much at face value.[37] The stabilisation strategy does not directly address the drivers of Yemen's downward trajectory but instead tacitly assumes the existence of an environment in which technocrats hold the reigns. Focusing on the technocrats assumes that the political barriers to their ascendance have already been removed.

CHAPTER THREE

The informal rules of the game

The tribes

The tribes are the most pervasive social forces in Yemen but their level of influence at the national level varies greatly depending on their proximity to the regime. Saleh's tribe (the Sanhan), for example, is small but enjoys tremendous access to state resources. It is from this group that the regime's inner circle (discussed below) is drawn. The Sanhan's significance has grown since Saleh took power in 1978; prior to that it was quite insignificant.[1] The Sanhan are members of the Hashid tribal confederation, which is the smaller but more internally cohesive of the two major northern tribal confederations, both of which are based in the mountainous areas that surround Sana'a. Both the Hashid and the Bakil (to a lesser extent) have disproportionate influence at the elite level, and at the lower levels of the tribal hierarchy, members have disproportionate access to employment in the military and security apparatus. This furthers the degree to which the regime's inner circle needs to include Hashid and Bakil elites' interests in their decision-making.

While perhaps only 20% of the total population considers their tribe as their primary unit of identity,[2] the tribes – and specifically their potential to engage in armed rebellion – are a significant factor in the regime's political calculations, and there is an element of mutual reliance between the regime and some tribal groups (particularly the Hashid and Bakil). Tribal militia groups have been raised to defend the state against external aggression on many occasions, including against the former South Yemen and Saudi Arabia, in the civil war of 1994, against domestic armed uprisings such as the al-Houthi uprising that began in 2004 and, more recently, against al-Qaeda. The *Small Arms Survey* reported in 2003 that Yemen's tribes held a total of approximately 5.58m small arms, and that the sheikhs personally held a further 184,000 or so, compared with the state's total of about 1.5m.[3]

While notional, this estimate clearly underlines the extent to which the Yemeni state lacks a monopoly on the legitimate use of force and is, therefore, partly reliant on the tribes for support, or at least acquiescence. The regime, therefore, has incentives to strengthen the tribes, while at the same time it fears them and is motivated to weaken them. This partial dependence was a feature of the political environment in which the Saleh regime operated. It has reduced the regime's short-term incentives to offer benefits horizontally through the tribes, creating a situation in which control is maintained by working through co-opted sheikhs. By fragmenting traditional power structures, possible threats from potentially powerful social forces are divided into more manageable segments. But in so doing, the regime has also weakened the legitimacy of the co-opted tribal sheikhs within their communities – an issue that AQAP has seized upon in an effort to further detach the tribes from the regime.

Many tribal sheikhs receive direct budgetary support paid as stipends through the Department of Tribal Affairs, an opaque organisation that is officially attached to the Ministry of Local

Affairs and which distributes money and benefits to tribal leaders deemed politically relevant by the regime. One tribal sheikh who received a monthly stipend from the Department described its careful application of carrots and sticks:

> The more [the sheikhs] get from the government, the more support they provide the government in doing what is asked of them. In some cases there are rebels in some tribes and the government can't intervene with the army, but they can ask the sheikh to suppress the rebellion ... Now all the big sheikhs get all the funds they want from the government. If he challenges the government, he will lose these benefits.[4]

The decisions about who receives these payments are not made as a matter of public record, and attempts by parliamentarians to determine the amount of money dispersed and the reciprocal expectations have been unsuccessful: 'They couldn't reply to my questions about how the money is distributed ... It is rather random and it depends on the influence of the tribe on the government, it is not distributed by merit, but by good relations with the government.'[5] As Paul Dresch observes, resentment has been steadily building against the fortune that the co-opted sheiks have amassed as the regime increased its reliance on financial co-optation rather than bargaining with local communities. One commonly hears tribespeople express the view that the shift towards cash incentives for sheikhs has been made at the expense of their local communities. As a consequence of these incentives, Dresch argues, even the more cohesive Hashid tribal confederation is unlikely to stand behind a sheikh as forcefully as it would have done in the 1970s.[6]

Until Yemen's oil era began the late 1980s, the nature of tribal leadership had been quite constant; the status of a tribal leader (sheikh) was based on a combination of heredity and merit, and the acceptance of that status within their tribe. In the oil-era, the regime of President Saleh intentionally provided incentives for loyalty, often at the expense of the sheikh's traditional obligation to promote the welfare of his tribe to the central authorities. The norms of tribal codes of conduct and conflict resolution entered a state of flux, being reinterpreted and renegotiated according to the selective favours offered by the Yemeni regime. As the wealth of the central state increased, so too did its ability to influence sheikhs in the periphery, many of whom relocated to the cities to manage their relations with Sana'a, which further distanced them from their tribal constituencies. As the ability of tribal leaders to draw wealth and status from the political centre increased, the bond between the sheikhs and their tribal constituents was loosened and the level of group solidarity within the tribes has diminished as a consequence. This has greatly increased the sheikhs' access to wealth but has simultaneously weakened the cohesion of their tribal support base which, over the longer term, reduces the political capital that they have to exercise against the regime. The rational desire of the regime to maintain power by undermining the threat posed by the tribes created the collectively irrational outcome of undermining its own ability to adapt to broaden its base of support against civil unrest.

Neopatrimonialism

The term 'neopatrimonial' is derived from Max Weber's discussion of three ideal types of legitimate political authority: legal–rational, charismatic and traditional. Patrimonial leadership, which Weber classes as a sub-set of traditional leadership, refers to a pattern of legitimate authority in which the leader 'regards all governing powers and the corresponding economic rights as privately appropriated economic advantages'.[7] A patrimonial leader exercises highly personalised authority and limits political violence by distributing benefits and/or status to the people. Weber contrasts traditional authority with rational–legal authority, wherein the leader governs through but is also limited by 'a consistent system of abstract rules which have normally been intentionally established'.[8]

This study follows a definition of neopatrimonialism advanced by Michael Bratton and Nicolas Van de Walle in their study of African politics. For them, it is a type of political authority that exhibits elements of patrimonial and elements of legal–rational authority, and which functions within the context of the modern state system.[9] Bratton and Van de Walle argue that neopatrimonialism in Africa has three primary characteristics: the concentration of power in the hands of the president, 'the systematic recourse to clientelism', and the selective distribution of state resources such as public sector employment, government licences, contracts and projects in exchange for political loyalty.[10] Each of these characteristics is evident in Yemen, where President Saleh governed and maintained his power through patron–client relations as opposed to law or ideology, and clients extended their political loyalty (or at least acquiescence) to him in exchange for benefits. In the Yemeni context, neopatrimonialism refers to the permeation of informal patrimonial loyalties into formal state organisations. Political parties, civil-society organisations, local councils and the parliament – organisations associated with a modern state – are used by the president in conjunction with traditional informal organisations to expand his patron–client networks.

While power may be concentrated in the hands of the president, this does not necessarily suggest that ordinary Yemenis see a system of personalised rule as inherently illegitimate. In Weberian terms, patrimonialism is a specific type of legitimate authority, which does not imply that the leader is necessarily ineffective or corrupt. A significant portion of Yemenis understand their socio-political reality through the lens of their tribe and there remains a strong sense that the nation is contained under the aegis of a single patron. However, there are complex reciprocities between patrimonial leaders and their subjects that cements their personal authority.[11] As the case of Botswana illustrates, neopatrimonial authority is not inherently incompatible with developmental leadership or democratic values, and can provide a stable basis for development in some political contexts, and under some leaders.[12]

In Yemen, there are complex ways in which President Saleh sought obedience and maintained his legitimacy over the course of his tenure. One of the most important of these was the promise of relative stability within a heavily armed society, and of being the provider of 'safe' and gradual processes of political and social change. For example, shortly after the 2006 presidential elections, he stated in a speech: 'The Yemeni people said "yes" to security and stability on September 20 [election day].' He went on to highlight the dangers of American intervention by asking: 'Which is better, Saddam Hussein's dictatorship or today's democracy in Iraq where massacres happen every day? ... Which is better, the dictatorship of Mohammed [Siyaad] Barre or the situation in Somalia now?'[13] The message was clear: the stability offered by dictatorship was preferable to state collapse, and his regime was preventing such a collapse. This is a message that resonated among an already vulnerable population.

Patrimonial leadership is a long-established form of public authority in Yemen. However, the rapid introduction of oil income into the political system also allowed the president to project an unprecedented level of centralised authority into the periphery. This deeply affected the basis of informal reciprocal arrangements between a Yemeni leader and society. Central power is now more visible than at any other time in Yemen's history. But was this rapid centralisation destined to produce a predatory and collusive style of leadership, or is it possible that a more developmental outcome might have been possible had it been chosen by the president and his regime?

The literature on neopatrimonialism tends to explain the sources of political malignancy, instability and violent conflict that often seem entrenched in this type of political authority. However, it has more difficulty explaining the ways that neopatrimonial regimes endure beyond their ability to coerce and co-opt.[14] To understand the softer power exercised by these types of regimes, and the agential behaviour that becomes entrenched through repeated action, it is important to look at the sources of legitimacy within the patronage system: which actors are included, on what basis they are included, and what are their expectations of inclusion?

The patronage system: the outer circle

The Yemeni patronage system constitutes the basis of the political settlement between Yemen's outer circle of elites, and is different to the political settlement that operates with the regime's small inner circle, which is discussed separately.

Yemen's patronage system is significantly shaped by the fact that the state does not maintain a monopoly on the legitimate use of violence and presides over a recently unified country that has already experienced civil war since it was established. As a result, the regime must exercise more caution than some of its regional counterparts when applying, or threatening to apply, physical force against influential political and social elites. The regime therefore places a high premium on complementing its coercive power with its ability to co-opt, divide, reward and punish these elites through the mechanisms of the patronage system. The informal, though implicitly understood extraction and delivery mechanisms of the patronage system constitute the 'rules of the game' for Yemen's elites. These principles have evolved (and been renegotiated) during the tenure of President Saleh, but they are underwritten by the fact that his close family members control the state's most important military posts and its ability to employ devastating physical force, particularly from the air.[15] These principles have also metastasised into a more predatory and collusive form since oil revenues began to dominate the country's GDP and the regime's incentives to bargain with society were reduced.

Who is included?

The most salient feature of Yemen's elite patronage system is its inclusiveness. Because patronage politics are so much more relevant in determining political influence and resource allocation than are the country's formal institutions, patronage must be accessible to all politically, economically and socially relevant elites. To be included, an elite must be able to demonstrate its relevance to the maintenance of the political status quo. This is an ongoing negotiation, and those who fail to establish their relevance lose their positions within the system. Not all elites are included equally and neither are they necessarily included permanently. Access to the system is not open to those whom the regime does not consider influential within a given constituency. With some important exceptions, most of those included in the system are not individually influential in key political decisions, but are included as a means of maintaining stability and regional diversity, and preventing elites from challenging the regime's inner circle.[16] The fact that so many people are enmeshed in the patronage system suggests that the structural constraints facing Yemeni elites are the sum total of the agents who maintain the system.

Tribal and military elites are systematically favoured within the patronage system over the business, technocratic and political party elites.[17] The tribal and military elites have benefited from the state's opaque processes of awarding contracts and procurement opportunities to such a degree that they have edged out many of the traditional merchants, and now dominate the business and investment sectors. The traditional merchants, most of whom come from the settled agricultural areas of Ta'izz, Ibb south of Sana'a, the large eastern governorate Hadhramaut and the city of Aden, lost the political influence that they once enjoyed in the aftermath of the 1994 civil war, when the northern regime elites consolidated their power. However, the economic influence of the traditional merchants ensures that they are not excluded from the patronage system. Finally, the political party elite is also included as a group in the patronage system, albeit to a lesser degree than the others. Technocrats are included as individuals but their interests are not considered critical to the regime's decision-making processes. Individual technocrats can, therefore, be excluded from state patronage but as a group their interests are still considered by the regime, and most can expect a level of benefits as long as they do not step over certain red lines in their work.[18]

The Yemeni system can be described as a 'limited access order', because access to organisations is heavily restricted for non-elites, which allows the elite to capture wealth, generate further rents and distribute benefits on a discretionary basis.[19] The provision of patronage to elites – according to the norms of which are discussed below – is critical to the regime's ability to contain violence and maintain its centralised rule but it also limits competition, retards economic growth and reduces the regime's incentives to enforce the rule of law. Yemeni power relations are fluid, and while the president must take the interests of domestic elites into consideration when making decisions, these elites do not constitute a static group and an individual can be included or excluded on what may seem a fairly arbitrary basis.

One of the participants in the survey articulated the closed nature of the system concisely, though apparently unintentionally; when asked what was the most effective way of getting things done in Yemen. He replied:

> A: Bribes, money and influence.
> Q: Is this way open to anyone?
> A: Yes.
> Q: Who can get things done this way?
> A: Anyone with money, power and influence.
> Q: Can/how can an outsider get things done?
> A: Yes, using all of these things.[20]

By this account, the ability to 'get things done' requires that an actor has 'money, power and influence' and is, therefore, not really an outsider to the game of elite politics.

In an article for the *Middle East Journal*, April Alley points out that the inclusiveness of Yemen's elite settlement carries the proviso that inclusion is not optional. Elites must accept a level of inclusion when it is offered or risk serious sanctions.[21] More than just the threat of punishment, however, is the understanding that refusing inclusion also means the likelihood of political isolation. Even among genuinely committed reformers, the preference has largely been for maintaining access to the regime, and the possibility for political action that this brings, rather than for taking a moral stance by defecting, although even before 2011 this was not unheard of. One leader in a minor political party commented that 'people are clever enough to realise' that rejecting the offer to cooperate with the regime usually means being entirely marginalised and thus losing the possibility of having even a very limited impact.[22]

The Yemeni case suggests that the higher the level of inclusiveness in a political settlement, the lower the common denominator between its constituents, which can make it more difficult to negotiate changes to the status quo. Instead, the political settlement becomes principally geared towards the distribution of rents and favours, and dissent is focused on the weighting of that distribution rather than on development issues.

Where are the red lines?

Former Yemeni Prime Minister Abdul-Qadr Ba Jammal commented in 2010 that '[a person] who can't be rich under President Ali Abduallah Saleh's regime can never be rich'.[23] Such were the rewards of showing one's loyalty to the president. The only strict red line within Yemeni patronage politics is that those whom it includes must not overtly challenge the system of elite corruption that underwrites the regime, to which they have at least partially acquiesced by accepting inclusion.[24] It is widely believed within Yemen that Saleh actually kept relatively reliable records of the corrupt activities of influential elites through the Central Organisation for Control and Auditing (COCA), a supposedly independent organisation that, in reality, reported directly to the president.[25] In the words of one source close to the president, Saleh was explicit in his distrust of people who 'do not steal', and used COCA to monitor government corruption as a way of 'putting a knee into the backs' of those who were disloyal to him through the threat of prosecution.[26]

One former head of COCA reportedly commented, as he looked over the vast body of evidence against government officials that his organisation had amassed over the years, that the COCA archives contained 'Yemen's secret history'.[27] Evidence of the intended use of COCA's audits is further indicated by the calibre of some of its top appointees, particularly that of the prominent Political Security Organisation (PSO) officer, Dr Abdullah Farawan. As Farawan awaited trial for transgressions that he allegedly committed while serving in the Public Prosecutions Office between 2000 and 2005, the charges against him disappeared and he was appointed as the head of COCA. Again allegedly committing major fraud during his time in this position, he was fired and indicted. As he awaited trial for the second time, the charges against him were once again dropped and, to the disbelief of most observers, he was appointed to head the Judicial Inspection Board to assist them in their efforts against judicial corruption and to ensure the integrity of judges.[28] Like its counterpart organisations elsewhere in the region, COCA is used to record the corruption of elites lest they overstep on the real red-line issue of challenging the corrupt political economy that supports the regime, and require legitimate grounds for punishment. It is not a body that is charged, in practice, with curbing official corruption; rather it channels that corruption into avenues that are acceptable to the regime.

A similar practice is employed with investors in Yemen, upon whom a corporate tax rate of 35% is levied, compared to 12% in Oman, 10% in Qatar, 20% in Saudi Arabia and 15% in Kuwait.[29] Despite Yemen's relatively high rate, only 7.3% of the country's GDP came from taxes in 2010.[30] The reason for this is that many companies keep two sets of accounts, one of which is accurate and another that is given to the tax authorities and shows negligible profits.[31] Some companies and individuals are also permitted to negotiate the level of tax that they pay to Yemen's authorities. The impact of this punitive tax base is to deter investment but, more importantly, it makes investors complicit in the criminalisation of the state. They become either guilty of tax evasion (and vulnerable to prosecution or blackmail) or are unable to compete in the market place.

It is acceptable for individuals to complain that corruption is the source of Yemen's economic and political malaise but it is entirely unacceptable for an individual or a coalition to build popular support for an alternative political-economic model. This helps to explain the regime's response to protesters who called in March 2011 for an end to the regime, and greater accountability and transparency. It is, therefore, acceptable to say that the government, or even the regime, is corrupt – which is sometimes a way of manoeuvring for a better position within the patronage system – but to take this to the next level by working to implement genuine solutions means defecting from the system. This is why, in the 2006 local and presidential elections, for example, the opposition coalition did not launch an official challenge to the results of the elections despite its initial (though exaggerated) claim that its candidate Faisal bin Shamlan received two million more votes than he was officially awarded. Instead, the JMP released a statement that it wanted 'to avoid a clash or confrontation with the authorities which [might] derail the process of change that has begun'.[32] The JMP therefore clarified that it was prepared to manoeuvre within the parameters of the system for gradual change and perhaps a stronger hand in future negotiations, but that it was not prepared to risk challenging for the presidency.

Rivalry

Yemen's elites also operate within a highly complex and intentionally opaque system that further limits the opportunities for collective action. The level and nature of the benefits that an individual receives are discretionary and may change either over time or very rapidly, which makes it difficult for an actor to confidently predict the likely outcomes of a given action. With each actor bargaining for a better position and no formal appeal mechanism, it is widely felt that sharing information can be dangerous. Secrecy is, therefore, an asset.

The actors included in the system were also constrained by the president's intentional creation of rivalries between players. If one player gained too much influence or otherwise made trouble, President Saleh could reinforce the strength of their opponents, something that was seen particularly in the way that he managed the tribes. President Saleh also had an incredible personal capacity for remembering tribal and familial networks, which is a valuable asset for a patrimonial leader. It is not uncommon for Yemenis who briefly met the president to report their amazement at his ability to accurately map their relatives once they reveal their full name to him. A common complaint, particularly among the tribes, is that the regime will fund or arm both parties to a dispute as a means of playing both sides against the middle and maintaining its own position of dominance. One sheikh from the governorate of al-Jawf commented to the *New York Times*, for example: 'The government plays divide and rule with us ... If one tribe will not do what [the president] wants, he gets the neighbors to pressure it. Sometimes it's money, sometimes it's weapons, sometimes it's employment for the tribesmen.'[33] A tribal source close to President Saleh confirmed this, noting that he encouraged tribal disputes for his political advantage: 'He gives [violent conflict] the green light, he lets them know that he will not stand in the way.'[34] Part of the president's resilience was derived from his ability to create (or stoke latent) divisions between those who might be capable of effectively opposing him and his inner circle. However, another part of his resilience derived from his role as a mediator in large conflicts. At times he worked to support ceasefires, as was seen in the support that he offered to the truce between the Bal Harith and Abeeda tribes in Marib in 2010. President Saleh was thus both a player and an adjudicator.

Crisis management

Finally, the benefits and obligations that inclusion in the patronage system entails can be expected to increase in times of crisis, which puts considerable upward pressure on the resources in the system. Solutions to problems are not created by recourse to an impartial arbiter but through the dispersal of resources, benefits and status. These goods are attracted by creating a crisis and then negotiating a solution with the leadership. The norms of the system are reasonably effective at containing, or at least channelling, conflicts but it does not enforce incentives to avoid conflict or, at least, the realistic threat thereof. For a player to maintain their relevance they must maintain their ability to create problems and/or solutions for the president. The focal point of this system is thus short-term: it is built to respond to immediate pressures in the system that can be targeted with money or other benefits; but longer-term systemic pressures are generally beyond the scope of a tool as blunt as the co-optation of elites. The implications of this for a rentier economy that is fast running out of oil revenue are both obvious and deeply concerning.

A striking, though by no means unusual, example of how funds are drawn from the state treasury and distributed to elites in an effort to quell unrest occurred in late 2007, when the southern protest movement had gathered unexpected strength and the Sa'da conflict had reignited. In November of that year, the total of the 2008 budget was announced to the media before the details were delivered to the parliament for approval. The stated total was $7.4bn. However, the total amount that was actually sent to parliament for approval the following day was significantly higher, at $9.15bn. The overnight increase came as a shock to those involved in the process and caused some frantic reorganisation to present the new figures for the final budget. Two ranking officials who were interviewed at the time explained that the sudden increase in the budget was due to the addition of $1.75bn in discretionary funds for the president to distribute to elites in the south and in Sa'da through direct payments and gifts. This was consistent with the $750m that the local press widely reported that President Saleh had spent on discouraging dissent in Aden at the end of 2007. That money was spent on handouts for elites, however, rather than on community development projects.[35] Shortly after the amended 2008 budget was approved, the minister of finance realised the need to cut costs elsewhere and issued a circular to all ministries that their operational budgets would be reduced by 30%.

This example illustrates that because the regime's feedback mechanisms are so unsubtle, quiet resistance is unlikely to be rewarded, whereas those who create crises are eligible for considerable rewards. Manoeuvring for greater rewards by creating crises is not perceived as threat to the system; in fact it legitimises the system by entrenching its structures through repeated behaviour.

Political economy

It is widely argued in the 'resource curse' literature that states with an abundance of natural resources are more likely to suffer developmentally, by experiencing poor economic performance, poor governance and violent conflict.[36] On the surface this appears to be the case in Yemen. However, the more important question is what political and social factors have also allowed the regime elite to use the sudden influx of wealth to enrich themselves at the expense of the population? Why have they been either unwilling or unable to use that wealth to promote development in the way that elites in some other developing states, such as Mauritius and Botswana, did?[37]

The answer lies partly in a coincidence of history that saw economic dominance transferred from society to the state, partly in the lack of perceived incentives for the regime to act otherwise, and partly in the collective action problems that the oil-based patronage system has instilled. In the first Middle Eastern oil boom, from 1973 until the early 1980s, North Yemen's per capita income increased by roughly three times, despite the fact that Yemen was not an oil-producing state at that time.[38] Instead, Yemen benefited from its large labour force that was earning money in the Gulf and sending remittances home. In the ongoing second major boom, the situation is very different. Even though Yemen is now an oil-producing state, there has been only a marginal increase in the country's per capita income. Not only have the record per-barrel oil prices not been trickling down to the population but there has been no similar outpouring of Yemeni workers to the much wealthier countries that surround it.

There are two main reasons for this. Firstly, unskilled labour was in much higher demand in the region in the mid-1970s than it is now, which favoured the mostly unskilled Yemeni labour force. Although Yemen has established a plethora of universities, the skills acquired by the graduates are either insufficient for or are simply not required by local or regional markets. The second reason relates to the unenviable position that Yemen was forced into when Iraq invaded Kuwait in August 1990, an invasion which occurred during Yemen's temporary membership in the United Nations Security Council (UNSC). The new Yemeni state could either support military action against Iraq, and damage the warm relationship between Saddam Hussein and President Saleh, or it could refrain from supporting military action and damage its relationship with Saudi Arabia and Kuwait. It chose the latter, and called for an 'Arab solution' to the conflict, which US Secretary of State James A. Baker III famously referred to as 'the most expensive "no" vote you will ever cast'.[39] Baker's warning was prescient: between

800,000 and one million Yemeni migrant labourers were hastily expelled from Saudi Arabia and Kuwait which, in addition to severing the billion or so dollars that they contributed in remittances annually, caused an extraordinary strain on the new state's fledgling economy. The impact of the returned unemployed labourers was further exacerbated by Yemen's loss of most of the development aid that it received, the vast majority of which had been provided by Saudi Arabia, Kuwait and, to a lesser extent, the United States.

As the amount of remittances entering Yemen plummeted as a result of this expulsion, the country's oil exports also increased dramatically. In a very short time the balance of power switched from a remittance-rich, relatively autonomous citizenry and a poor state, to a poor and relatively economically dependent citizenry and an oil-rich state.[40] In short, it was not just the influx of oil income that centralised Yemen's wealth but the fact that this change occurred almost simultaneously with the restrictions to citizens' ability also to access rentier income from abroad. This two-sided shift on the interests and incentives of the president and his inner circle are reflected in the renegotiation of the political settlement between the regime and Yemeni social forces in favour of the former.

This also shifted the location of the country's economic elite. Prior to the influx of oil wealth in the early 1990s the majority of Yemen's contractors were from around Ta'izz (with a few from Ibb, al-Baydha and Marib) but the ability of the Saleh regime to distribute economic largesse to its traditional clients has meant that there are now only two major contractors from the area. Under the current political settlement, the merchants of Ta'izz are politically marginalised but they are still economically powerful. The Hayel Saeed Anam Group of Companies warrants special mention; it is Yemen's largest private sector company, and the country's only truly multinational company.

It is pragmatic and has solid business ties in both Saudi Arabia and in the regime's inner circle.

However, while the state-sponsored patronage system has been built largely on access to oil income since unification, rents are also received in strategic payments from other states, and from the centralised revenue that *qat* farming brings, the lion's share of which is captured by sheikhs in the *qat*-producing areas.[41] The most important outcome of this shift is that scarcity at the lower levels of society does not necessarily mean scarcity at the top as long as access to rents are maintained. Finally, the regime's ability to access security assistance, training and high-tech weaponry from external sources also helps to shield it from the costs of repression.[42] The Yemeni regime, therefore, has several buffers through which it secures its political and economic independence from society.

To transition to a post-oil economy, Yemen would need to attract considerable foreign investment, something that the government has acknowledged repeatedly, but for which it has granted very few resources. The level of political risk attached to investing in Yemen, combined with the high levels of corruption and the weakness of formal state organisations to enforce the law and protect investors, make it very costly to do business there. Contracts are frequently not honoured or are subject to continued renegotiation, and the lack of formal organisations means that foreign investors are reliant upon the personal contacts of their agents, which is difficult, if impossible, to maintain oversight of. Extortion is widespread and there is little reliable recourse for investors. The amount of foreign investment beyond the oil and gas industries, therefore, remains negligible, and there are few indications that this is likely to increase significantly in the short term.[43] As April Longley and Abdul-Ghani al-Iryani note: 'Since the April 2007 Yemeni Investment Conference in Sana'a, the government has announced investment promises of over $260 billion [nearly thirty times the then national budget]. The absurdity of this figure is matched only by the almost complete absence of credible investment.'[44] By the end of 2009, the announcements had reached a total of around $310bn despite the fact that there was no significant new interest even in the most recent bidding rounds for oil and gas acreage.

One incident vividly illustrates the obstacles to attracting foreign investment: just a day before the Investment Opportunities Conference in Sana'a in April 2007, that is, after most of the delegates had already arrived, there was a gunfight just 100m south of the presidential palace between Yasser al-Awadhi (a member of parliament from al-Baydha) and his tribal entourage, and one of the top sheikhs from Sanhan. At that time Awadhi was deeply embedded in the president's network.[45] Nobody was injured, despite the fact that the shooting continued for many hours, creating a public spectacle in which the roads around the palace had to be closed to traffic, all of which suggested that the incident was largely posturing.[46] Two days after the conference there was a similar, though more violent incident, in which shooting erupted between two parties that were also embedded in the regime's inner circle: the commander of the Republican Guard in Ta'izz (Abdul-Lateef al-Dhaneen – the son of the Sanhan sheikh, Saleh al-Dhaneen), and the Republican Guard in Sana'a (commanded by the president's son). The fighting was apparently over Dhaneen's attempt to seize property in Sana'a that was owned by the president of the United Arab Emirates. Several soldiers were killed and the incident created another very public spectacle. Gunfire from this second conflict continued intermittently for two days despite the fact that it was actually between two friendly factions of the Republican Guard. Speculation was strong within business circles that the violence was orchestrated to illustrate to investors the need for local protection against such threats. This incident suggests that the agential constraints to a productive economy are at least as robust as the structural constraints.

The climate for foreign investment is further undermined by President Saleh's insistence that the shadowy and unaudited Yemen Economic Corporation (YECO, formerly the Military Economic Corporation, or MECO) be the local partner for prospective investors.[47] The corporation, which is run by Ali al-Kohlani, the uncle of one of Saleh's wives,[48] was granted vast tracts of public land in Sana'a and Aden, and named the local partner for the Dubai-based real estate developer Emaar to develop properties on that land. Just before the 2007 investment conference, Emaar publicly stated its intention to invest a minimum of $1bn in Yemen. However, the president's insistence that Emaar partner with YECO caused the company to withdraw its plans.[49] At the time of writing, Emaar has not returned to invest in Yemen.

If we assume that the president and his inner circle are rational actors, then these examples of apparently intentional sabotage highlight the importance of agency in Yemen's failure to diversify its economy beyond rentier income. This suggests that there was a collective perception within this group that their interests were better served by maintaining the economic status quo, which is essentially the point that Robert Bates makes regarding the lack of necessity for political elites to nurture their domestic economies if rents remain available.[50] Chapter 5 will examine the role of foreign actors in reinforcing the perception that bargaining with the international community is more lucrative than bargaining with Yemeni society.

Collective-action problems in the patronage system

Yemen's patronage system is fuelled by elite graft. While the main instruments to fuel the patronage system have changed over the years, it is now based on the misappropriation of funds (through smuggling and paper transfers) of the large diesel subsidies. A patronage system can be useful for maintaining political stability and limiting violence in the short term, but it becomes unsustainable if the common resources are overexploited. As Yemen's oil reserves depleted, and the amount of money flowing through the system dropped, why was collective restraint not being exercised in the enlightened self interest of those who benefited from the goods that the patronage system delivered?

The parable of the 'tragedy of the commons' helps to explain the collective-action problem that the patronage system entrenches. In the social dilemma of the tragic commons, popularised by Garrett Hardin (1968),[51] a group of famers has access to a common grassed area upon which to sustain their individually owned herds of sheep. Each farmer, being rational, wishes to keep as many sheep as possible on the commons in order to make more money – the sheep being a mechanism for converting common property (grass) into individual wealth. However, if the grass is consumed faster than the rate at which it grows (because the number of sheep is unsustainable) the farmers are collectively disadvantaged. The dilemma is that a farmer who adds extra sheep to the commons receives all of the profit, while the cost of doing so is distributed to the group. Each farmer, therefore, has an individual incentive to increase their use of the land even though doing so reduces the productivity of the land, and affects them all adversely. The selfish, though rational, short-term individual preferences of the farmers undermine their longer-term individual interests. Furthermore, the agential behaviour of the farmers creates structural barriers to collective reform because once one farmer overuses the common resource without being punished the action becomes legitimised. The rational behaviour of individuals can thus create collective irrationality.

Solving this collective-action problem is typically understood to require either the conversion of the common resource into privately owned property (the exploitation of which is, therefore, regulated by the private owners because they have incentives to maintain its productivity), or through the creation of a public authority that is capable of regulating the amount of the common resource available to an individual.[52] But there is also another option: that the farmers lobby wealthy landowners from the neighbouring village to give them more land and more grass and thus prevent an outbreak of violence between the famers that may affect those beyond the borders of the commons. However, this does not solve the collective-action problem because farmers are still rationally inclined to continue to overstep their quotas, but the farmers and the neighbouring landowners may both perceive that granting the land is a short-term circuit breaker for impending violence. If the farmers are confident that the threat of a conflict spill-over is sufficiently threatening to their neighbours, there is a disincentive for them to pursue the two longer-term solutions to their collective-resource problem, even though it is more likely to create longer-term security for all players.

CHAPTER FOUR

External geopolitical actors

Saudi Arabia

> The most common response of Yemeni citizens in the
> informal setting of *Qat* chews to the question 'how is
> Yemen going to get out of these problems' was 'we'll
> blackmail our neighbours.[1]

The Kingdom of Saudi Arabia exercises more influence in
Yemen than any other external actor. The two countries share
a long and porous border – a frequent source of anxiety for
the Saudi government, which fears an influx of militant jihadis,
contraband or refugees from its impoverished southern neighbour. As the competitiveness between Saudi Arabia and Iran
increases, the kingdom is also concerned that its rival may
gain a foothold on the peninsula through Shia proxies operating close to the Saudi border. As previously discussed, the
al-Houthi insurgents (Shia muslims, mostly from the northwestern provinces of Yemen, who follow the Zaydi school of
Islamic jurisprudence) have sporadically fought the government since 2004.[2] Both Yemen and Saudi Arabia (though

particularly the former) accuse the Iranian government of supporting the insurgency. Despite these accusations, neither the Yemenis nor the Saudis have publicly offered any concrete evidence of Iran's alleged support.

Believing that Yemen's political instability exposes the kingdom to a range of serious threats, the Saudi government has pursued a three-pronged approach towards its neighbour. The first is containment using a combination of physical barricades, high-tech border-monitoring equipment, buffer zones and military action. The second is the offer of financial support to the regime to protect it from economic collapse, and the third involves a more scattergun attempt to purchase influence or more likely, the possibility of spoilers, from sub-state actors in Yemen. This third prong is particularly obvious within Yemen's northern tribes, although some security sources have noted that the Saudi government has also offered direct payments to some members of Yemen's military.[3]

Saudi policy towards Yemen is opaque, ad hoc and sometimes contradictory, but one generalisation can be made: the overriding objective is to contain Yemen's problems within Yemen and to prevent them from spilling over the border. An adviser to a senior Saudi Prince summarised this position succinctly when he told Ginny Hill of Chatham House: 'We don't care what they do, as long as it's stable.'[4] In other words, the kingdom views the possibility of significant change in Yemen as threatening and so has worked to support the status quo of power hierarchies, however economically unsustainable they may be in the longer term. It is here that Saudi Arabia's policy appears most contradictory: how does the simultaneous provision of money to the regime *and* the regime's potential detractors support stability? The answer is that Saudi Arabia understands stability and political power in Yemen rather differently to the way that Western governments and donors tend to understand it, and that it also has a more realistic understanding of the weight that Yemen's informal power structures have. Where Western governments have focused on trying to enhance the capacity of the formal state to increase Yemen's stability, Saudi Arabia has focused on supporting the networks that constitute the informal state to maintain the status quo. For Saudi Arabia, engaging with Yemen's informal institutions and power centres legitimises a political system that does not threaten its own domestic political arrangements.

As was discussed in Chapter 3, Yemen's informal political settlements exacerbate economic malaise but have been relatively durable, in part because they have created such formidable barriers to change. In supporting these settlements the kingdom has, intentionally or otherwise, kept Yemen significantly dependent on its financial largesse, thereby preventing it from posing a significant challenge to its position as the peninsula's hegemon.

The relationship between the two states is fraught, and ordinary Yemenis often hold Saudi Arabia responsible for many of Yemen's domestic problems.[5] While a tendency towards conspiracy theories is a common feature of polities where access to reliable information is restricted, there is some basis to popular suspicions over the role of Saudi Arabia in Yemen. It is widely held that factions within the Saudi regime had sought not only the independence of the south but also the establishment of a state in Hadhramaut in 1994. Despite the fact that Saudi Arabia did not recognise the breakaway southern state – the Democratic Republic of Yemen – in 1994, two justifications for this view are often cited in Yemeni political circles. The first surrounds kingdom's strategic interest in gaining free access to the open sea to ease the passage of its oil exports. After signing the border treaty with Yemen in 2000, Saudi Arabia proposed a plan to build a pipeline through Yemen's large eastern governorate of Hadhramaut to the port of Mukalla, and insisted on having sovereignty over a 20km-wide corridor of Hadhramaut – a request that was refused by the Yemeni government.[6] A report by the Gulf Research Center (a Saudi-funded research institute based in the UAE) in August 2007 suggested that this interest has been revived, due partly to the strategic threat posed by Iran in the Gulf.[7] However, Saudi Arabia does have the capacity to transport oil internationally from ports in the Red Sea, and is also pursuing a pipeline that would terminate in the UAE, which means that Yemen is not the only option for it to obtain access to the open sea. The second justification is that the kingdom is home to a small but highly influential minority of Saudis of Hadhrami origin, and is concerned with the long-term security implications of this group maintaining divided loyalties. Families such as the al-Amoudi, Buqshan, Ba Hamdan, bin Mafouz and bin Laden all constitute massive mainstream economic powerhouses in Saudi Arabia. Sharing that divided loyalty with a satellite state of Hadhramaut, rather than with a large and potentially hostile state of Yemen, might be a less threatening option for the kingdom. While neither of these factors proves that Saudi Arabia did actively support southern secession in 1994 (and less that it would do so again), they underline the level of involvement that Riyadh maintains in Yemen, and the popular resentment that this provokes within Yemen.

Prior to 2000, the annual discretionary budget that the kingdom granted to the body that administers Saudi–Yemeni relations, the Special Committee for Yemeni Affairs (SCYA) was extremely high: approximately $3.5bn (SR13bn). It has since been reduced and accurate figures could not be obtained at the time of writing. To give some indication, however, the Saudi government confirmed in 2008 that the monthly stipend of $800,000 that it had been paying to Yemen's paramount sheikh, the late Sheikh Abdullah bin Hussein al-Ahmar, would be paid instead to his sons.[8] Under the border agreement between the two states finalised in 2000, all Saudi funding was to be channelled through the Yemeni government instead of being paid directly to the tribes, but despite this arrangement the independent payments continued. Unofficial estimates of the number of people in Yemen currently receiving subsidies from Saudi Arabia remain in the thousands, which highlights the importance that Yemen's largest neighbour places on maintaining leverage across the border. While Saudi Arabia funds tribes in other neighbouring states as well, including Iraq and Jordan, the amount of money that it pays to Yemeni tribes is far greater than what the Yemeni regime publicly admits to spending on the tribes which, in 2005, was just over $5m per annum.[9]

Many within Yemen believe that the money being channelled by Saudi Arabia into Yemen is increasing, but it has not been possible to obtain a clear macro-level picture of how much is being distributed or who the individual recipients are, other than the obvious figures within the regime. In the words of one source who receives regular payments from Saudi Arabia: 'everybody can get money from Saudi Arabia if he knows someone there, or if he is a sheikh or even just a tribesman ... they give money to Hashid, Bakil, Madhaj, everybody, all tribes of Yemen receive money from Saudi Arabia.'[10] The journalist Dexter Filkins cites a similar source in April 2011:

> Tribal leaders receive even more money from the Saudi government ... Abdullah Rashed al-Jumaili, a sheikh in the Baqil [sic] tribe, told me, 'I take a salary from the Saudis as well as from the Yemeni government. Well, it is not so much a salary as a gift.' Jumaili

said that he received about twenty-seven hundred dollars a month from the Saudis and twenty-three hundred dollars from the Yemeni government ... 'All of the sheikhs receive this money,' Jumaili said. 'It's the system.'[11]

Another significant indicator of the level of money the kingdom is pouring into the grassroots of Yemeni society was the lavish display that Saudi Arabia made to mark the anniversary of the north Yemeni revolution on 26 September 2010. The streets around the Saudi embassy were closed for several hours as Yemeni citizens waited to collect money directly from the embassy.

After the end of the 'sixth war'[12] in Sa'da in February 2010 (which directly involved the Saudi military), more than 50 Bakil sheikhs were invited to meet Crown Prince Sultan bin Abdul-Aziz in Saudi Arabia, and again more names were added to the list. One day after this meeting, President Saleh travelled to Saudi Arabia unexpectedly to meet with King Abdullah. Saleh was accompanied by the minister of defence, the head of national security and General Ali Muhsin. Observers within Yemen noted that the haste with which this trip occurred pointed to the Yemeni regime's concerns that Saudi Arabia could have been mobilising tribal leaders against it. It appears that this was not, at least immediately, the case but it indicates the level of potential threat that the Yemeni regime perceives from Prince Sultan's faction in Saudi Arabia.[13]

While it is beyond the scope of this chapter to discuss the nature of the Saudi regime in any detail, it is important to mention that its factional rivalries are at least partly being played out in Yemen, and there are two competing views within the Saudi regime about how Yemen should be dealt with. King Abdullah's faction has been willing to channel large amounts of money directly to President Saleh in the apparent hope that helping to bankroll his survival would help to prevent Yemen's problems from reaching Saudi Arabia. Prince Sultan and Prince Naif (and their sons, Khalid bin Sultan and Mohammed bin Naif respectively) are believed by many in Sana'a's political circles to entertain ideas of securing access to the Arabian Sea through the western part of Hadhramaut, as discussed above.[14] However, it has not been possible to determine whether this is a serious desire or simply an assumption of ongoing malicious intent. These divisions in the House of Saud over its Yemen policy were described in a US diplomatic cable leaked through WikiLeaks, which states:

> The prolonged absence from Saudi Arabia of Special Office chairman Crown Prince Sultan ... who [redacted] claims is also highly skeptical of Saleh, left the Yemen file in the hands of King Abdullah, who has greater confidence in Saleh's motives and leadership abilities. Committee members have kept their doubts about Saleh's leadership abilities private since the departure of Crown Prince Sultan, creating a vacuum of Yemen policy advice in the Saudi Government that resulted in the decision to intervene directly in the Houthi conflict, [redacted]. King Abdullah was much more receptive to Saleh's entreaties for direct Saudi involvement than Crown Prince Sultan ever would have been...[15]

President Saleh has long operated under the conviction that the possibility of state failure in Yemen poses too big a threat to international security for the West to allow it to occur. However, Saudi Arabia has thus far proven the most receptive to this tactic. In 2009, the kingdom made a direct payment of $2.2bn to President Saleh and the United Arab Emirates followed suit with $700m,[16] making the total (known) amount around two-thirds of what Yemen earned from oil exports when revenues peaked in 2008.[17] This is largely what allowed the government to pay the civil service and military wage bill and prevented a major economic crisis in 2009. This view was corroborated in a cable released through WikiLeaks, which notes that the American Embassy in Riyadh says: 'We agree ... that Saudi support is enabling Saleh to weather increased domestic political pressure.'[18]

In August 2010, Saudi Arabia again contributed funds directly to the Yemeni Central Bank, just one month before the 'Friends of Yemen' group of international donors met in New York. The influx of foreign currency was apparent when the value of the Yemeni riyal reached its lowest point ever (YR257 to the US dollar) at the beginning of August, only to recover to YR231 by the end of the month. A local economist estimated that this change in the exchange rate required an intervention of at least $1bn.[19] Estimates by donors and diplomats of the amount that was donated by Saudi Arabia ranged between $1–2bn.[20] The provision of this money undermined the unity of purpose that the Western members of the Friends of Yemen had hoped to display. More importantly, however, this payment points to the differences between Saudi Arabia's concept of stability in Yemen and the concept that is held by Western governments. While the latter attempt to exert influence through Yemen's formal state mechanisms, Saudi Arabia understands that the real power exists within Yemen's shadow state, and so it is with the shadow state that the kingdom exerts its influence. In helping to maintain the power hierarchies of the shadow state, Saudi Arabia's actions also undermine the developmental model being advocated by Western donors.

In addition to the money the Yemeni regime has received from Saudi Arabia, Yemen's minister of finance spent about a week in Libya in October 2010, negotiating a fixed deposit of $500m in the Central Bank to redress the balance of payments. It is widely believed that while this money could be withdrawn, it is most likely to remain a grant if the relationship between Yemen and Libya remains amicable.[21] It appears that President Saleh believes that these closed-door payments will continue as long as his neighbours deem the threat of Yemen's collapse sufficiently serious.

The West

President Saleh (like many Yemenis) apparently believed that Yemen is simply too important for the West or its neighbours to allow to fail. Since the attempted bombing of an American passenger jet on Christmas Day 2009 was traced to al-Qaeda in the Arabian Peninsula (AQAP) in Yemen, the Yemeni government has been trying to convince foreign donors that it requires extraordinary financial assistance to stay afloat in the face of the terrorist threat. In 2010, for example, requests for aid by the Yemeni government ranged from $1.2bn to a staggering $44.5bn over five years, or over half of the country's current annual national budget every year for the next five years.[22] Similarly, Yemen's Foreign Minister Abu-Bakr al-Qirbi called for a 'Marshall Plan' of some $40bn. While these requests dramatically overstate what the Yemeni government could actually be hoping to receive, the logic employed is quite indicative of the regime's incentives to act.

These incentives are further indicated by the fact that by January 2010, only 7% of the $4.7bn pledged by donors at the 2006 conference in London had been spent.[23] The Yemeni government argues that this is because it lacks the technical capacity to absorb the funds, and this point was highlighted in the leaked McKinsey report that developed the Ten Point Plan. However, the obstacles are again not only related to structural capacity, but are also strongly related to the president's preferences. A member of the cabinet revealed in an interview that neither he nor any of his counterparts in other line ministries ever received the letter from the Ministry of Finance to advise them of what their ministry's allocation of the funding would be, which meant that no action could be taken.[24] If the ministries were never instructed that they would receive the money, it is not simply a matter of their incapacity that prevented it from being spent; it is a matter of will. This, combined with President Saleh's attempts to convince the IMF to give direct budget support instead of balance-of-payments support, strongly suggests that government capacity is not the only limiting factor in its ability to absorb development money. The president's ability to choose not to accept the conditions attached to that money is also a significant factor.

The United States is the most influential Western donor in Yemen and the financial assistance it has offered has increased significantly – though far less dramatically than requested – since the attempted Christmas airliner bombing in 2009, to approximately $130m per year in non-security assistance (up from approximately $22m in 2008).[25] Similarly, the British budget for development aid in Yemen 2010/2011 increased by 43% to £50m.[26] These figures show that the amount of financial support available from the West pales in comparison to what is available more locally, particularly when the conditionality of that assistance is also taken into account.

While the Yemeni regime usually states that what it needs from the West is financial and developmental support, the imbalance in what it actually receives from the West and what it receives from its neighbours suggests that what it really wants from the West is legitimacy. International legitimacy is thus an Achilles' heel for President Saleh, as it will be for whoever follows him, which makes the West's policy options look quite different to the ones currently being pursued, in which the Yemeni regime is to be 'stabilised' above all else.

CHAPTER FIVE

The regime

The inner circle

The informal and fluid web of power created by President Saleh to consolidate his family's power is best described as a series of concentric circles with the president at their centre. Tightly wrapped around the president in the next concentric circle are his close relatives (sons, nephews, half-brothers, cousins and in-laws), and slightly further away is the elite of the Sanhan tribe. These three circles, consisting of perhaps 50 or so actors, constitute the regime's inner circle. Some of its members control the country's most sensitive military positions. Their family backgrounds are rural, and those in the public eye have had limited formal education other than what they gained during their time serving in the military. There is nothing to indicate that the rest of the inner circle – that is, those not in serving the military – is any different in terms of their level of education.

The inner circle is an extremely shadowy group and there are conflicting reports about the precise identity and familial relations of those within it, as well as the number of members, other than those recognisable through their prominent posi-tions within the military or relationship to President Saleh.

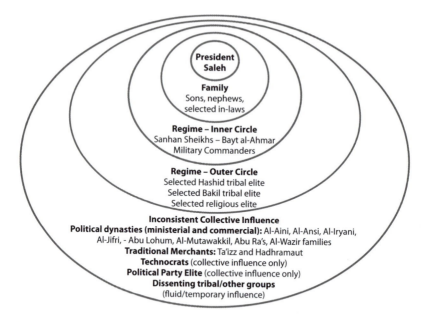

Even within the regime's inner circle there are different – and fluid – levels of inclusion afforded to different actors, ranging from those whom the president cannot easily exclude from important decisions against their will, to those whom he can exclude from some important decisions against their will.

President Saleh is from Bayt al-Ahmar, a village of about 15 households in a poor rural area approximately 40km outside of Sana'a. In a pun on the place name, which is also a reference to the dominant Hashid family of sheikhs – the al-Ahmars – Yemenis often note that the country's next leader will be from one of two places: Bayt al-Ahmar (the president's home village) or Bayt al-Ahmar ('the household' of the sheikhly al-Ahmar family).

It is widely accepted that President Saleh was trying to groom his eldest son, Ahmed Ali Abdullah Saleh, to succeed him. Ahmed is, however, unpopular among ordinary Yemenis. As a result of this – and President Saleh's apparent recognition that his succession was untenable – his ambitions appeared to shift to his much younger son Khaled, who

graduated from Sandhurst Military Academy in the UK in
2010. Within the inner circle, Ahmed controls the Republican
Guard. The force consists of some 30,000 men and a vitally
important military unit that was consciously modelled on its
Iraqi counterpart.[1]

Saleh's daughter Bilquis, who was once married to his
nephew Yahya, wields considerable influence within the
palace and is believed to have an impressive economic port-
folio. President Saleh's half-brothers, nephews, cousins and
in-laws also form the core of the inner circle's public face.
They include Air Force Commander Mohammed Saleh
al-Ahmar, the president's half-brother; Director of the Office
of the Commander and Chief Ali Saleh al-Ahmar, another half-
brother; Deputy Commander ('Staff Officer') of the Central
Security Forces Yahya Mohammed Abdullah Saleh, a nephew;
deputy commander of the National Security Bureau 'Ammar
Mohammed Saleh, a nephew;[2] and Head of the Presidential
Guard Tariq Mohammed Abdullah Saleh, a nephew. These
positions, though particularly those commanded by his son
Ahmed and his nephew Tariq, were essentially tasked with the
protection of President Saleh's personal leadership. A younger
generation is now also emerging and includes the commander
of the Missile Forces, Khaled Ali Abdullah Saleh, the president's son; and Tayseer Saleh Abdullah Saleh, military attaché
in Washington, the president's nephew.

The country is divided into five military zones, all of which
are controlled by either relatives of the president or members
of the Sanhan elite. The only exception is the Central Military
District, which is officially under the command of a southerner,
Saif Saleh al-Boqari, but in reality Boqari is only a figure-
head and the district (which includes the capital of Sana'a) is
controlled by the president. The other district commanders are:
Ali Muhsin al-Ahmar (no relation to the sheikhly al-Ahmar

family), commander of the 1st Armoured Division and the North Western Military District, the most politically significant of the commanders; Mahdi Maqwallah, commander of the Southern Military District (which includes Aden), who derives his power from his close association with President Saleh;[3] Mohammed Ali Muhsin, who commands the South-Eastern Military District (which includes Hadhramaut);[4] and Abdullah al-Qadhi, commander of the Ta'izz Military District. All four men are members of the Sanhan tribal elite; Qadhi has the added distinction of being the head of the powerful al-Qadhi clan. In early March 2011, Abdullah al-Qadhi was the first from his group to defect when he declared his support for the protest movement against Ali Abdullah Saleh, apparently in retaliation for the attempted assassination of his son, Mohammed (a member of parliament) by Central Security forces on 8 March.[5] The attempt on Mohammed's life was believed to be retribution for his close relationship with Hussein and Hameed al-Ahmar, two of Sheikh Abdullah's more prominent sons, whose political ambitions have helped to fuel a long-standing acrimony with President Saleh and his family. As is discussed later, al-Qadhi's defection was followed shortly afterwards by that of Ali Huhsin, the most powerful member of the regime's inner circle.

Ali Muhsin has a level of support within the military that ensured his leverage with the president, and that his economic interests were taken seriously. His economic holdings are impressive, if difficult to pinpoint exactly. He holds a majority share in at least two of the country's nine national banks, owns a number of companies that provide local representation for foreign oil companies (in exchange for a percentage of their profits), and a number (estimates vary as to exactly how many) of tanker ships upon which subsidised diesel is smuggled from Yemen to neighbouring countries.[6]

Muhsin is a distant cousin of the president, but has usually been considered the second most powerful figure in the country. His military power was considerably reduced during the Sa'da wars: sources close to him have stated that by late 2010 the 1st Armoured Division numbered just 2,000 soldiers out of a previous 20,000. However, his political influence remained formidable and he was never considered to have been out of the political game permanently.

Ali Mushin goes by the last name al-Ahmar (a reference to the village that he is from) but he is generally believed to be from the al-Qadhi clan. A source close to members of his family claims, however, that Ali Muhsin's real last name is Jaabr. Like most of the inner circle, he is a shadowy figure relative to the power that he wields. The fact that even his full name remains unclear underlines the level of opacity that exists within the Sanhan elite. While most Sana'a residents could easily point out Ali Muhsin's residence on Sixty Metre Road,[7] until a few years ago most also reported never having seen a photograph of him. As a further example of the level of knowledge that is publicly available about the members of the regime's inner circle, many reports previously in circulation in Yemen wrongly said that Ali Muhsin was President Saleh's half-brother. The two men are both from the Sanhan tribe, and both are from the village of Bayt al-Ahmar. While Ali Muhsin is not a Sanhan sheikh, his al-Qadhi descent puts him higher than President Saleh in the Sanhan tribal hierarchy. As is discussed below, Muhsin's increasing public appearances over the past few years seem to be related to the factional rivalry between himself and the president, which led to efforts to undermine his political influence in favour of Saleh's closer relatives.

Internal palace politics are the source of continual debate and rumour within Yemen's political classes, but these debates tend not to be based on verifiable evidence. Saleh actively prevented members of the Sanhan elite, other than a selection of his close relatives, from appearing in the media. The author is not aware of any publicly available photographs of his half-brother Ali Saleh ever having been published. His other half brother, Mohammed Saleh, makes only very rare media appearances: even though he is much more powerful than the minister of defence, it is the minister's picture that is in the public domain. The regime also intentionally keeps the names of the inner circle out of the public realm, and until several years ago even President Saleh's last name – 'Afaash – was treated as though it were a state secret. It is likely that this was because the name revealed that President Saleh is not a sheikh, and does not come from a respected tribal pedigree. Because of this intentional opacity, it has not has not been possible to gather a list of all of the names of the members of the Sanhan inner circle.

There are six significant families that come from the president's village of Bayt al-Ahmar: 'Afaash, al-Akwa, Najar, al-Qadhi, al-Dhaneen and Jaabr. Between these families (probably comprising about a few hundred people), there are two main factions, the 'Afaash clan (those related by blood to President Saleh) and the al-Qadhi clan (those related by blood to Ali Muhsin). While firm lines are difficult to draw, 'Afaash, al-Akwa and Najar families are considered to be largely loyalists to President Saleh, while the al-Qadhi, al-Dhaneen and Jaabr families are considered to be loyalists to Ali Muhsin. Since about 2000, President Saleh and his sons and nephews have attempted to undermine the influence of the Sanhan old guard – particularly the al-Qadhi and al-Dhaneen families – using tactics of intimidation and humiliation.[8]

Another small group worthy of mention in the regime's inner circle is comprised of three men who have almost unparalleled access to the president but who are not members of the

Sanhan and, therefore, could never come into conflict with any other member of the inner circle. These are Ali Shatter, head of the military publishing company Tawjih al-Ma'anawi; Abdo Burji, deputy director of the Office of the President;[9] and Abdullah Bashiri, head of the Presidential Secretariat. Their roles are essentially that of a political kitchen cabinet. They are personally liked and trusted by Saleh and play the important role of gatekeepers in a system in which everything runs on the personal micromanagement of the president.

Succession and factional rivalry

The political struggle over who should succeed President Saleh has not been particularly significant in the external view of Yemen in the first decade of the twenty-first century, but it has been of paramount importance domestically. The question of who will lead Yemen after Saleh and, by extension, what the basis of their political legitimacy will be, has coloured the background of most high-level domestic politics throughout this period.

It is widely believed, including by sources close to both the president and to Ali Muhsin, that the struggle for political succession constituted one of the many layers to the conflict in Sa'da between government forces and a group of insurgents led by the al-Houthi family.[10] Ali Muhsin and Saleh were long-time allies, but they were also each other's biggest rivals, and it is clear that the competitiveness between them started over the question of political succession, although it is not clear that Ali Muhsin actually believed that he should have become president himself. Hameed al-Ahmar (the son of Sheikh Abdullah) stated in an interview on al-Jazeera in late 2009, for example, that the Sa'da war was largely a war over political succession: 'the Republican Guards headed by the President's son supported the Shi'ite rebels in north Yemen in order to hit the

1st Armoured Division led by Brigadier General Ali Mohsen [Muhsin] Al-Ahmar and hence get rid of him … a rebel leader is a friend of the President's son, Ahmad Ali Abdullah Saleh.'[11] The governorate of Sa'da is located within Ali Muhsin's area of military command (the northwestern region), and what began in there in mid-2004 as a fairly local conflict, based on largely political grievances, developed into an ongoing series of wars that have since embroiled the regime.[12] However, the sections of the military commanded by Muhsin bore the brunt of this conflict.

In April 2007, a source close to the president noted in an interview that Saleh had informed Ali Muhsin that he would not be given any new military hardware to pursue the war in Sa'da, despite the fact that the Republican Guard continued to procure weapons from Russia at the time.[13] The same source said that as the conflict expanded, Muhsin had also requested support from the Republican Guard (controlled by the president's son Ahmed Ali) and the Central Security Forces (controlled by Saleh's nephew, Yahya Mohammed Abdullah Saleh) but that his requests were refused. Despite the Republican Guard's reputation as the most elite section of the Yemeni military, the president chose instead to mobilise brigades with capabilities inferior to the Republican Guard and the Central Security Forces. Many politically aware Yemenis interviewed by the author at the time, portrayed this choice as illustrating the president's desire not to tarnish either Ahmed Ali or Yahya in the Sa'da conflict, and to instead weaken Ali Muhsin in an unwinnable war. Regardless of whether this was the intention, the outcome was that Ali Muhsin was weakened by his ongoing involvement in Sa'da.

In the 'sixth' Sa'da War (August 2009 – February 2010) the roles changed and the Republican Guard did fight, while the 1st Armoured Division stood back and instead surrendered 11 military bases without a major battle and without destroying their arms depots. There was widespread speculation this time of collusion between the al-Houthis and Muhsin's division and that these weapons were actually sold to the al-Houthis to fight the Republican Guard, indicating Muhsin's intention to regain ground lost to President Saleh.[14]

How the inner circle's political settlement was forged

The mechanisms by which a political regime is created often remain deeply embedded in the institutions that it uses to maintain its power.[15] Yemen's organisationally weak, person-alised webs of loyalty, which helped Saleh rise from military command to take power after the assassination of President Ahmed al-Ghashmi, form the basis of the inner circle's polit-ical settlement. In 1978, as commander of the Ta'izz Military District, Saleh had access to Bab al-Mandab at the mouth of the Red Sea, which provided him with lucrative interna-tional smuggling opportunities and meant he was the second highest-ranking Sanhan military commander. (The highest ranking commander, Mohammed Isma'il al-Qadhi, was then in the political wilderness.) Ali Muhsin was in charge of the Central Command Headquarters, which served as a Ministry of Defence. After the assassination, he secured the Headquarters building and held the chief of staff, Abdul-Aziz Barati, in a locked room while he waited for other Sanhan commanders to build enough support within the military for Ali Abdullah Saleh to take control of the building, thereby making him supreme commander of the military.[16]

The standoff continued for 40 days in June–July 1978, during which time the speaker of parliament, Abdul-Kareem al-'Arashi, served as acting president. Throughout this period, several non-Sanhan military commanders attempted unsuc-cessfully to seize the headquarters. The acting president was also entertaining the possibility of remaining as president until his house was attacked and sprayed with bullets. During the 40 days of political uncertainty, as the Sanhan elite were selling their assets and gathering cash in support of Saleh's attempt to capture the presidency, an agreement was reached between the tribal elites who were involved. It was referred to as 'the covenant' (al-'ahd). Essentially the inner circle's political settlement, it contained an understanding that the Sanhan tribe would stand together under the leadership of Ali Abdullah Saleh and that Ali Muhsin would be next in line to succeed Saleh as president.[17] The succession line did not extend beyond Ali Muhsin and it is likely that, knowing the short-life span of other republican presidents, the adherents to 'the covenant' did not expect their leadership to endure very far into the future. It was widely reported, for example, that when Saleh took office a CIA agent in Sana'a took bets that he would not last six months. In other words, Saleh's presidency (and the Sanhan ascendance) was reasonably expected to be a short-term proposition. Despite its hasty creation and short life-expectancy, aspects of the Sanhan political settlement went on to be renegotiated as the ambitions and strategies of the players changed.

The issue of political succession lay largely dormant until 1999, when President Saleh began to push for a series of politically regressive constitutional amendments. One of the amendments in the package was an extension of the presidential term of office from five to seven years. Even though he had been in office since 1978, President Saleh was only officially elected for the first time in 1999, meaning that that under the amended constitution he could now remain in office until 2013, instead of 2009. This prompted intense speculation that this was intended to allow the president's son Ahmed Ali Abdullah Saleh to reach the age of 40 – the constitutional minimum age for a Yemeni president – before President Saleh was compelled to retire.

Some of the elite within the president's tribe, including particularly Ali Muhsin, were reportedly outraged at the president's apparent attempt to position his son to succeed him, and this sparked a major factional dispute, though not necessarily because Muhsin wanted the top job for himself. One of Muhsin's most powerful supporters, the commander of the Eastern Region, Mohammed Isma'il al-Qadhi, spoke out and, according to a Sanhan insider, explicitly told President Saleh that he was 'breaking the covenant'. Very shortly after this reported conversation, in August 1999, Qadhi was killed in a military helicopter crash.[18] Although the crash was officially declared an accident, this remains disputed, and is widely believed to mark the beginning of other more subtle moves against Muhsin within the military, and other officers and units loyal to Muhsin that began be to removed or weakened.[19]

A collective-action problem

The crucial distinction between President Saleh and the rest of the regime's inner circle has been that he was the only member of the group that had legitimate constitutional power.[20] He was the lynchpin of the political system and the charismatic leader of the state for two generations.[21] This conferred a level of legitimacy upon his leadership that his inner circle could not access. While many Yemenis did not always approve of the way that he ruled, most still accepted him as their legitimate president, at least until March 2011. The same cannot be said for his shadowy inner circle of Sanhan elites which, while providing the coercive muscle for President Saleh, are mostly unknown to the Yemeni people, partly because the president so actively prevented them from appearing in the media or in public.

The power of the inner circle derives from their control of the military, from the economic wealth that they have amassed through predatory practices and, most importantly, from the level of access that their positions within the Sanhan tribe granted them to President Saleh. Lacking any constitutional or legitimate power themselves, the biggest threat to those in the president's inner circle has been the possibility of changes to the predatory and collusive rules of the game from which they have all individually benefited. If the president were to increase his reliance on the rule of law to foster private investment and economic growth, they would not only forgo their short-term financial interests but would also risk becoming less politically relevant to him in the longer term. The only way around this dilemma would be if the members of the inner circle were to have collectively bought into an economic model that increased the possibility of growth for themselves *and* the citizens, but so far they have shown no appetite for this. Such is the threat that the inner circle has perceived from Saleh's ability to use rational-legal authority at their expense, that members of Saleh's 'Afaash clan have been known to defect to Muhsin's al-Qadhi clan when Saleh replaced military leaders within the inner circle using legal procedures rather than consultation. In mid-2009, President Saleh used his formal power to remove Sanhan heavyweight Mahdi Muqwallah from his post as the commander of the Southern Military District. Saleh appointed his nephew Tariq in Muqwallah's stead, but was forced to restore Muqwallah within in a month due to concerted pressure from the rest of the inner circle. They were not prepared to accept Saleh using his legal authority to override the informal rules of the game in which members of the inner circle could not be removed unilaterally.

A further indication of the way that formal power is seen as a breach of the informal settlement came when Ali Muhsin made his first foray into the media spotlight, at a time when he was being squeezed particularly hard by President Saleh over the war in Sa'da. In September 2007, it was announced that Ali

Muhsin had established a new research institute, the Yemeni Centre for Historical Studies and Future Strategies, the main goals of which are to evaluate the problems affecting national stability and unity. The centre's 206 board members included four senior technocratic advisers to President Saleh, 30 opposition parliamentarians, five serving ministers, six former ministers, five governors and five former governors.[22] At least two of the four senior advisers were never consulted, and their names were simply added to the list. In a seemingly symbolic gesture, Ahmed Isma'il al-Qadhi was also appointed to sit on the board of the centre. Ahmed is the brother of Mohammed Isma'il al-Qadhi, who was killed in 1999 in the helicopter crash. Ali Muhsin appeared on national television for the first time, wearing a suit, which was seized upon by politically aware Yemenis for the obvious break with normal operating procedures – and for the symbolic challenge to President Saleh – that this represented.[23] Operating through more formal and open channels was thus seen and popularly understood as an explicit challenge to Saleh by breaking the norm that the inner circle should be neither seen nor heard.

If we assume that the regime's inner circle, as rational actors, do not wish to lose power by succumbing to uncontainable civil unrest, or by suffering a total economic collapse once oil reserves are depleted, then it has been in their interests to take decisive action. It is not in their collective interests to sponsor the erosion of their own longer-term legitimacy by further entrenching the country's problems for short-term rewards. However, the transition to a post-oil economy requires that each member sustain a significant loss to his present levels of power, wealth and ability to dispense patronage and so each has been individually disinclined to do so. The members of the inner circle were less likely to maintain their exceptionally privileged positions if they pursued reforms that promote greater prosperity among the population, because such reforms would have required a reliance on the rule of law, which would have limited their access to power and wealth. The benefits of such reforms, if they accrued to the regime at all, would have accrued to President Saleh at their expense. It would have increased the president's reliance on his rational-legal authority over his reliance on his patrimonial authority. As is seen in some other authoritarian regimes, it is individually rational for the members of the president's inner circle to block the emergence of a political system based on the rule of law that may facilitate the emergence of a post-rentier economy, and thus their own longer-term survival. It is, therefore, also individually rational for the members of the inner circle to continue to behave in an economically unsustainable manner. However, this is all based on perception and competition; if perceptions change and a threat to their collective survival emerges, then calculations of individual rationality are also likely to shift, although not necessarily to a more developmentally-inclined paradigm.

Within the rules of the game, President Saleh essentially held a veto power against any individual within his inner circle, but when the inner circle united it was able to challenge him, and so it too held a collective veto power over the president.[24] The president and his inner circle have been thus mutually reliant and similarly, though not identically, constrained.

The Yemeni regime

Expanding outwards from the Sanhan elite are the fluid networks that constitute the wider Yemeni regime, which are organised informally through the mechanisms of the patronage system. The next circle of elites is incredibly influential and can still be considered part of the regime's core; it contains a network of tribal elites that are critically though not necessarily individually important in the president's decision-making. The

Hashid tribal confederation is the smaller but more cohesive and powerful of Yemen's two major tribal confederations. The Bakil confederation is roughly four times the size of Hashid in number, but many of its members are isolated and there are several contenders for the position of Bakil's *shaykh mashaykh*, or paramount sheikh. This position is undisputed within Hashid and is held by Sheikh Sadiq bin Abdullah al-Ahmar, who is the eldest son of the Hashid leader Sheikh Abdullah bin Hussein al-Ahmar, who died in December 2007.[25] While it can be argued that only a small percentage of Hashid members benefit directly from the current political order, favouritism towards Hashid is still said to be rampant when it comes to allocating lower positions in the civil service and military. Northern tribal sheikhs (even those outside of Hashid and Bakil) can be considered to be members of the regime collectively insofar as their interests are considered, however, with the exception of the al-Ahmar family, the Sanhan sheikhs and some of the major Bakil sheikhs (such as Sheikh Abu Lahoom, Sheikh al-Ghaadir, Sheikh Abu Raa's and Sheikh al-Shaif), they are not individually members of the regime.[26] The military-commercial elite is drawn mostly from these tribal groups and, along with the inner circle, it controls the Yemeni economy.

Among other noteworthy figures within the regime is Hameed al-Ahmar. While Hameed is not the *shaykh mashaykh* of the Hashid confederation, he is probably the most politically savvy of Sheikh Abdullah's ten sons,[27] and has been increasingly active in the Islah Party and the JMP since the 2006 elections. He is the most outspoken of the al-Ahmar family, despite the fact that his interests continued to be considered by the president throughout the period where their relationship was visibly tense. He remained an important figure within the regime although he was never a member of the inner circle. In fact, Hameed's willingness to criticise the president was probably more indicative of his relative safety within the regime's networks than it was a call for systemic change. He did not explicitly challenge the system of elite graft from which he benefited so substantially. By being so outspoken, and by increasingly funding the activities of (and the personal stipends of members within) the JMP, Hameed increased his influence within the opposition. Elements in the JMP were wary of him because of his reputation for corruption, his role in the 1994 civil war against the south, and for remaining entrenched in the regime establishment that he decried. However, having Hameed as a patron for the JMP better equipped the coalition to play at the table of elite politics with the regime. Hameed also maintained strong relationships with President Saleh's factional rivals in the Sanhan tribe – most notably Ali Muhsin – and has a very solid relationship with Yemen's key external patron, Saudi Arabia, from which he receives a monthly stipend.[28]

Another important Hashid figure is Hussein al-Ahmar, a younger half-brother of Hameed, who has become one of Saudi Arabia's most trusted political allies within Yemen. Hussein came to prominence in September 2007 when he established the National Solidarity Council, a tribal association dominated by sheikhs from all over the country. Hussein has raised tribal militia to fight the Houthis in Sa'da and has offered to mediate in the conflict. His erratic and contradictory positions seemed to indicate his perceived need to remain visible, and were probably an indication of his broader political ambitions. He has a reputation for being a tribesman first and a politician second – a reputation that may have helped to insulate him from some of the charges that were commonly levelled against his brother Hameed.

Placing the opposition leader Abdul-Majeed al-Zindani in a list of regime members is somewhat controversial, because he has moved in and out of favour with the president over time. His inclusion here underlines the ambiguous position of popular Islamist figures within the patronage system. Zindani, an influencial cleric and the rector of al-Iman University, had been very closely aligned with President Saleh in periods of tumultuous change in Yemen's recent history. After unification, Zindani was appointed as one of the three northerners in the five-member Presidential Council, the body that was replaced in 1994 by the Majlis al-Shura, or consultative council. While his influence has waned, he has provided an important link to Yemen's more radically inclined Salafis. His standing with Yemen's many thousands of Afghan returnees allowed him to muster a fighting force in defence of President Saleh in the 1994 civil war.[29] Further, in 2006 when the United States began in earnest to pursue Zindani for allegedly funding al-Qaeda, it was the president that provided him with protection while his party, Islah, stood more nervously on the sidelines.

President Saleh expected Zindani in return to deliver his Salafi constituency when needed. As tensions flared over the Sa'da war in July 2008, for example, Zindani established a Committee to Prevent Vice and Promote Virtue, which was styled after the Saudi Arabian *muta'wa* ('religious police'), and held a mandate to prevent what it deemed un-Islamic behaviour.[30] The committee forcibly closed several Chinese restaurants and black-market alcohol vendors. But the move quickly trespassed on the interests of the military, members of which make enormous profits from alcohol smuggling. Shortly afterwards, the Virtue Committee was reined in with the sale of black market alcohol quickly resuming and the restaurants re-opening. In October 2010, President Saleh turned to Zindani again to establish the Religious Reference Committee, which was granted control over 'all matters of public concern, large and small' in a presidential decree. While this committee ulti-mately came to nothing, by granting it control over the 'national dialogue' that the JMP had been pursuing with the GPC since 2006, appeared to be deliberately inflammatory.[31]

Independent business leaders are notable in their absence from this list largely because, since unification, business has been increasingly funnelled into the hands of the 'tribal capitalists' and the 'bureaucrats in business' who distribute the economic largesse of the state 'according to political criteria'.[32] According to these political criteria, independent business leaders are much less of a consideration than traditional clients. Similarly, technocratic or intellectual advisers are not consulted in any consistent fashion and their personal interests are not weighted nearly to the extent that the favoured tribal and military clients are. However, several political dynasties warrant mention: members of the Abu Lahoom, al-Ansi, Abu Ra's, al-Jifri, al-Iryani, al-Mutawakkil and al-Wazir families have managed to maintain a level of political relevance, whether through close collaboration with the regime, through positions as technocrats, through trying to push the boundaries of political reform, or complex and fluid combinations of these positions.

CHAPTER SIX

The political parties

The JMP[1]

In 2011, as the anti-Saleh protests gathered momentum, Western media and policymakers focused on Yemen's formal political opposition – the JMP – and the possibility that it could provide an alternative to the regime. An opinion piece in the *Guardian*, for example, described JMP leaders as 'doing everything in their power to bring demonstrators all over Yemen under the JMP umbrella … With that sort of adept political sense, the JMP may just steal the show without ever having to sleep in a protest tent in front of Sana'a University.'[2] This misrepresents the development of the protest movement, which began outside the auspices of the JMP and, in some ways, was also a protest against the entanglement of parts of the JMP – particularly Hameed al-Ahmar – within the regime.

The JMP is a diverse coalition of six opposition parties: Islah and the Yemeni Socialist Party (YSP) – the larger and more experienced, the Nasserite Party, the Union of Popular Forces (UPF), the al-Haqq Party and the Ba'ath National Party (also known as the Iraqi Ba'ath Party). The Ba'ath Party rejoined the JMP in 2009 after a brief period supporting the government in the 2006 elections; before that it was a member of the JMP from 2002 until 2006. The JMP's two largest members both have previous experience in government: the YSP ruled the People's Democratic Republic of Yemen (PDRY) from 1972 until 1990, and then governed the united country in coalition with the GPC until the 1994 civil war; Islah served in a coalition government with the GPC from 1994 until 1997.

Islah

Islah combines a number of Islamist schools of thought, but its Salafi and tribal leaders – who were so instrumental in the party's establishment in 1990 – have seen their power decline since the 1994 civil war. As the personal relationships deteriorated between the al-Ahmar family and some of its other elites on one hand, and the president on the other, the party became more detached from the state-sponsored patronage system in which it was once a pillar. However, in so doing, it increased its reliance on figures like Hameed al-Ahmar for protection, and continued to pursue secretive and exclusionary negotiations behind closed doors.

Islah is by far the largest and best organised party within the JMP; it has a considerable grassroots support base and a strong record in charitable work, which helps it to penetrate further into the fabric of society and extend its influence beyond the elite level. As an Islamist party, it also offers the only ideological alternative to the status quo. Beyond the very broad label of 'Islamist', however, it is difficult to attribute any one coherent ideological stance to the party. Religion provides more of a vocabulary to the party than a framework for decision-making or policy formation, and pragmatic political considerations have increasingly trumped theological concerns in Islah's public rhetoric. At the time of publication Islah held 46 of 301 seats in the parliament.

The YSP

The YSP's weight within the JMP is far greater than its membership numbers warrant. While the Islah party now has more members in the former south than the YSP, the YSP still has some historical legitimacy with the GPC, due to its experience as a governing party, as the GPC's partner in national unification, and as a 'symbol' of the south. Symbolism and history are powerful forces in Yemeni politics, particularly if the end goal is to negotiate for change rather than to compel it by sheer weight of numbers. The YSP's presence in the coalition, therefore, broadens the JMP's elite network considerably and lends it the credibility of political experience. Being the only other major party in Yemen, it is also the logical partner for Islah under an opposition umbrella; without the YSP, the JMP would be little more than a vehicle for Islah. In the parlament that was elected in 2003, the YSP held seven seats.

The Nasserite Party

The Nasserite Party holds just three seats in the parliament, but its weight among the JMP leadership is considerable. As an example, despite having a membership of only around 18,000 (2008 estimate, compared to an estimated 900,000 for Islah[3]), at least one representative from the party was almost always included in meetings conducted by the author with the coalition's leadership throughout the country in 2008. The party's only significant strongholds are in Dhala'e and Ta'izz, which are also key strongholds for Islah and the YSP.

Like the other two smaller parties in the coalition, the Nasserite Party has never been a significant player in the patronage system. Formerly an underground movement, its roots are in resistance-style politics and this is probably the party's most important contribution to the coalition. The fact that the Nasserite Party was never a part of the patronage system also helps the JMP demarcate space for itself outside that system, despite the fact that Islah and the YSP were once openly included as parties.

Hizb al-Haqq

The al-Haqq Party has no parliamentary representation, but as a Zaydi party that is informally led by descendents of the Prophet (the Sayyids) it holds some symbolic power, as well as some pockets of tangible – and apparently increasing – support in the northern governorates of Sa'ada and Hajja.[4] Such is the party's religious status that it was awarded the Ministry of Religious Endowments (*Awqaaf*) by the GPC, after the latter won a majority in the 1997 parliamentary elections. This ministry had previously been held by Islah.

Hizb al-Haqq has gained some news coverage since 2004 because Hussein al-Houthi, the instigator of the Believing Youth uprising in Sa'da, represented it in parliament from 1993 until 1997. Al-Haqq may be broadly sympathetic with some of the aims of the al-Houthi family, but it considers them a renegade group, not a formal faction of the party. Despite the party's official distance from the Sa'da conflict, events in the area have further distanced al-Haqq from the regime and have helped to reinforce the overall perception of defection from and resistance to the regime that the JMP has attempted to portray. However, al-Haqq has become more significant as a result of the successes of the Houthi insurgency in Sa'da in recent years. People are rejoining the party in the Zaydi areas north of Sana'a, although there have not been any parliamentary elections held since this time to measure the impact of its popularity more directly.

The Union of Popular Forces (UPF)

Like al-Haqq, the UPF is a Zaydi party but it exists almost entirely as an elite movement and has virtually no grassroots membership. The party's influence comes largely from members of its elite that live abroad, particularly in the United States and Saudi Arabia, and their ability to gather funding from and exert lobbying influence from abroad. Other than its elite networks, the UPF's relevance to the JMP is, like the other two minor partners, in spotlighting the coalition's defection from the regime and thus reducing the likelihood of re-assimilation by its members.

The (Syrian) Arab Ba'ath Socialist Party

The Ba'ath Party is also electorally insignificant, holding just one seat in parliament, which is unofficially 'reserved' for its general secretary, Abdul-Wahab Mahmood. The party has been closely historically aligned with the GPC, but it defected to the JMP in 2009, which underlined the JMP's identity as an alternative coalition to the GPC.

Why was the JMP established?

On the surface, the JMP was established out of the desire to compete more effectively with the GPC. Beneath the surface, however, a more defensive motive emerges. The JMP wants 'strength in numbers' protection from an authoritarian ruling party; its members hope that the regime is less likely to play them off against one another, or adopt coercive measures if they can present a united front, preferably one that has international legitimacy. Furthermore, a number of JMP participants made it clear that they wished their opinions to be directly conveyed to the international community by the research team. The JMP has provided its smaller members with protection from the regime, and in return the smaller parties have added legitimacy to the JMP's rhetoric of political exclusion, and have helped to provide evidence that Islah and the YSP – both previously in coalition with the GPC – have now fully defected from the regime. However, the only real requirement for JMP membership is not being a member of the GPC, and its members' historical backgrounds thus span the political spectrum, from the extreme left to the extreme right. Because there is little ideological glue to bind them together, it remains possible that any member could defect to the GPC.

The JMP is also burdened by the historical animosity between its senior coalition members, Islah and the YSP. Grassroots members of each were periodically involved in violent conflict throughout the 1970s and 1980s, which peaked when the two sides faced off in the 1994 civil war. The grassroots enmity between Islah and the YSP's respective support bases, particularly pronounced around Ibb, Ta'izz and Aden, had a significant impact on the coalition's performance in the 2006 local elections. Still feeling the scars of previous conflicts, areas sympathetic to Islah in and around Ibb and Ta'izz were reluctant to offer support to the YSP, and parts of the former South sympathetic to the YSP did not want to support Islah. These historical divisions are less important within an opposition movement, but if key positions in government become available, the JMP will be challenged if it is to maintain its unity without losing what remains of its support base.

The JMP's collective-action problem

The JMP's collective-action problem is the result of two factors. The first of these stems from the fact that the coalition contains such a diversity of political, ideological, tribal and religious views, and the recent memory of civil war between coalition's two largest parties (Islah with its origins in northern Yemen and the YSP with its southern origins). The umbrella offered by the JMP is so wide that there is even an extensive array of opinions regarding how best to approach the GPC, which ranges from close collaboration to complete defection.

In an effort to maintain the united front that its members believe is so important negotiating with the GPC, the JMP's central-level politics are built on compromise and a willingness to make concessions between one another (as individual elites) in order to reach a consensus and maintain the coalition. For example, the JMP's internal coalition bylaws state that no action can be undertaken unless every member party agrees to it; in reality, however, the decision is made by a narrow group within the leadership of each party. Every party thus has a veto on any collective action. While this is intended to maintain unity and prevent internal factionalism, it also places a limit on what can be achieved. If the interests of the individual parties are not in line with every other member's interests, the bylaws explicitly favour the lowest common denominator of acceptable action. This preference for maintaining the appearance of unity has had the effect of weakening all of the members by enforcing a sometimes bland uniformity.

A subset of this problem derives from the fact that Islah has vastly more popular support than any of the other parties, who see this as a threat to the unity of the coalition. There is a fear among the smaller partners that Islah party will ultimately emerge as the sole beneficiary of the coalition. The smaller parties fear marginalisation and eventual irrelevance; Islah, for its part, is concerned that its partners could withdraw from the coalition on the basis of that fear. Islah has thus agreed to a power-sharing agreement in which it is, theoretically, equal to its partners despite the problems that this causes for the coalition's overall strength. The reality of Islah's dominance in resources and organisational capacity is not openly acknowledged for fear of causing divisions.

In reaching this settlement, its members have also settled on a lowest-common-denominator basis of agreement in order to stay together. In avoiding some of the more loaded political issues, such as the role of women and sharia in political life, the basis of agreement has been set around calls for a sometimes ill-defined political and economic reform initiative. While genuinely held by the majority of the JMP, these goals also represent the JMP's endeavour to create a new inclusive ideological banner for itself in the absence of other value positions. There is no coherent policy, ideology or vision that links the parties together other than the broad desire to serve in the regime's stead and to implement a swathe of reforms about which the public has little clarity. There is no other internal political settlement within the JMP.

The second factor that limits the JMP's collective action is its elite status and hence its place in the network of informal power. It was conceived as a defence mechanism against the ruling party, but as an ideologically fragmented umbrella group for elites, it also mirrors some of the GPC's structural constraints. Developmental rhetoric has been a significant part of the JMP's survival strategy. Its central leadership implicitly views the purpose of the coalition as a mechanism for lobbying the government for greater concessions to a reform-minded elite, rather than as a means of gaining power or compelling change through the weight of its supporter base. Of course, the JMP is seriously constrained by the regime's deliberate efforts to undermine it at every step, but its popularity has also been hindered by its decision to limit its action to attempts to persuade the regime to change itself, rather than engaging more directly with citizens.

While the JMP's leadership decries the regime, it continues to eschew direct appeals to the street for fear of crossing the regime's red lines, engaging in populist politics and being either marginalised or crushed by the regime as a consequence. The JMP's reluctance to take this path is a rational response to its very difficult position, but the adverse effect on its popular credibility is clear. In its *Vision for National Salvation* (March 2010), for example, the JMP articulated many well-known diagnoses of, and technical solutions to, Yemen's political and economic crisis, and yet it has still failed to persuade the regime to either accept it as a partner for change, or to implement some of the reforms that it has recommended. One of the JMP's most senior leaders, when asked which of Yemen's problems the JMP had the ability to solve, put it bluntly: 'None, the JMP is just an umbrella to regenerate the legitimacy of the system.'[5] This leader was essentially articulating the widely held suspicion that the JMP's strategies have legitimised the closed-door and exclusionary bargaining favoured by the regime, at the expense of engaging with the ordinary Yemenis.

Dissatisfaction with the regime may be visible on the streets, but it is not being funnelled through the JMP. Evidence of this has been seen in protests in the south since 2007, in Ta'izz and, to a lesser degree, in Sana'a. The coalition, and particularly Sheikh Abdullah's outspoken son Hameed al-Ahmar, is widely seen as being enmeshed with the status quo. Its calls for political reform therefore have seemed esoteric and insincere to a public that does not see the links between its public rhetoric and improvements to their daily lives.

The JMP and elite bargaining

The neopatrimonial paradigm is ingrained in many aspects of the JMP's existence, and the fact that it reflects the system from which it has symbolically defected has presented the coalition with its greatest dilemma. The JMP has called loudly for progressive change and for the creation of a national unity government, but the structure of the JMP is still best suited to lobby-style politics, rather than to consolidating an alternative power centre.

The JMP has focused on trying to persuade President Saleh to enact reforms that benefit the opposition without making a sustained and focused effort to challenge him for his job. The most obvious incentives for this strategy are that it is less politically and economically costly. The JMP cannot realistically summon the level of resources that the GPC can and so it must make do with trying to maximise its position through bargaining and persuasion. For example, the concessions made by the regime prior to the 2006 elections (in an agreement known as the 'June 18 Agreement')[6] were, at least theoretically, greater than what it would have been forced to concede in an electoral contest. On paper the June 18 Agreement commits the GPC to a 'dialogue' (al-hiwar) on national reform in partnership with the JMP. However, the fact that the conditions under which such a dialogue may begin to proceed were still being negotiated in 2011 before the uprisings began points to the lack of perceived incentives for the regime to participate.

Furthermore, the JMP has not consistently challenged the logic of the neopatrimonial decision-making that continues to exclude it from the hierarchies of power (that is, decision-making by 'big men' with personal links to the regime who are beyond public scrutiny). One Islah member responded to the Developmental Leadership Program questionnaire that the reason the JMP is not more effective is because 'there is fear that any escalation will lead to confrontation'. He also commented on the lack of internal transparency within his own party, saying: 'I just want one true electoral cycle where democracy is practised within the party', indicating that a significant part of the problem is that the member parties of the JMP do not have the internal transparency/democracy that they call for in their opponent. Despite its claims to the contrary, the internal structures of the JMP largely mirror those of the GPC, and the desire to become more broad-based and inclusive seems absent from its vision. The JMP's actions and its ongoing preference for elite dialogue over grassroots populism suggest that while it wants different outcomes than those that prevailed under Saleh's rule, it is less certain that it wants an end to patrimonial politics. This said, the 2011 uprising and the fracturing of the elite have put Yemen in uncharted territory and the JMP's strategies and preferences could shift, but in so doing they would be altering their historical tendencies significantly.

One illustration of the JMP's preference for patronage-based strategies is that, since 2006, some parts of the JMP became outwardly concerned with seeking shelter under the protective umbrella of one of the regime's more outwardly rebellious members, Hameed al-Ahmar. Hameed has bankrolled many of the JMP's activities, provided some of its members with salaries and established the Preparatory Committee for National Dialogue. The Preparatory Committee has established a presence in the JMP's local branch offices and is working to try to increase grassroots support for the coalition, but the power of the central elite has remained dominant. As noted in Chapter 5, Hameed's presence in the JMP has been divisive,[7] because he is so unpopular in the south and so entangled in the regime's networks of corruption and privilege. One JMP participant in the DLP survey argued: 'Hameed thinks that we will be under his control but we know that he is no different to Saleh. We will never be under his control.'[8] However, in the absence of alternatives, Hameed's patronage presents an alternative to a coalition that is continually frustrated by the regime. In an interview with both Hameed and his older brother Sadiq al-Ahmar days after Ali Muhsin's defection from the regime, journalist Abigail Fielding-Smith noted that:

> A certain sharpness creeps into [Hameed's] tone when it is suggested that some of the protesters want to challenge the very structures of tribal power and wealth distribution at whose apex he sits ... 'The only

thing anyone has a right to ask for is a real democracy,' he says… [Sadiq also noted that] 'The youth are part of Yemen and they are sons of tribes … We don't want anyone changing these traditions.'[9]

As a coalition, the JMP challenged who was included in the system, but it only inconsistently challenged the nature of the system itself. This is not to say that there are not some members of the JMP who genuinely seek to create a political system that uses its wealth more productively and is more inclusive of average Yemenis, but that there is a fundamental mismatch between this goal and the norms of Yemen's political processes that the JMP has not, to date, been willing or able to consistently challenge.

The ruling party: the GPC

While the GPC has held the parliamentary majority and has long been considered Yemen's 'ruling party', Yemen has not in effect been governed by a formal political party. The GPC was a vehicle for the personalistic system of President Saleh; it has not exercised independent political power. Saleh established it as a permanent body in 1982 in an attempt to formalise the existing system of patronage that was available to politically relevant supporters of his rule. It was also intended to undermine the increasing political power and capacity of the Local Development Associations (LDAs). The LDAs emerged in the 1970s as civil-society organisations that used unregulated labour remittances to provide education and basic infrastructure (such as roads, schools, health facilities and water pipes) to communities beyond the control of the central government. Kiren Aziz Chaudhry argues that LDA spending between 1973 and 1980 was more than three times larger than the government's development spending during the same period – and was certainly much more effective. Concerned by the overt independence of these organisations, however, the government combined them in 1978 to form the centralised Confederation of Yemeni Cooperatives,[10] which began the process of their marginalisation. The establishment of the GPC finalised the co-optation of LDAs by the Saleh regime. As Sheila Carapico notes, the GPC's first Permanent Committee was made up of 700 delegates that had been elected to positions within the LDAs; President Saleh nominated another 300 members.[11]

These origins reveal much about the nature of the contemporary GPC. The party retains the ideological incoherence that justified its foundation, when political parties were banned and an incorporative political umbrella was the preferred method of accommodating competing political factions.[12] To be a member of the GPC, therefore, requires no necessary ideological leanings. Members and leaders are able to pursue various personal and business interests. While personal, military and tribal affiliations are very important in the competition for resources distributed by the president, the party quite happily incorporates people from very different ideological backgrounds on the strength of its own patronage system. Islamists, former socialists, merchants, tribal leaders, moderates, hard-line religious conservatives and some genuinely progressive reformers all exist side by side under the GPC umbrella.

The GPC was essentially created as a political mobilisational tool for the state and is a semi-formal shell in which the Saleh regime's patronage networks operate. The party is granted inordinate access to public money and the security apparatus, which explains the majority of its strength. Without its privileged access to the resources of the state and its role in their distribution, the party would cease to exist in its current form. Even when the party began to devolve some of its limited institutional power to the geographic periphery in the lead-up to the 2006 elections, it did so by targeting local traditional elites, members of the state security apparatus and district local council directors as new party members, not by appealing to the people with its policy platform. Restructuring in this way helped the GPC to better harness the input of local elites but showed that the party was still firmly founded upon the person-alised patronage system. As a party, the GPC is weaker than the sum of its parts and derives most of its power from being the party of the president. The GPC essentially lends support, and its parliamentary majority, to the will of President Saleh and, by extension, to the elites with whom he consults.

Why the political party elites have not acted developmentally

The 2010 DLP survey revealed a striking level of agreement between participants, whether from the opposition or the ruling party, that the country faces a serious threat. Not even the most cautious and embedded participants responded nega-tively to the question 'do you believe that there are serious problems facing Yemen?' Furthermore, all but one participant (a member of Islah) reported that 'the overall level of threat posed to Yemen's future' was either 'serious but temporary' or 'insurmountable and permanent',[13] with 79% electing the latter to define the nature of the threat. Almost two thirds (64%) of participants indicated that they believed that 'these problems will affect the daily lives of ordinary Yemenis' to a 'catastrophic' degree.

Furthermore, the majority of participants saw the causes of the problems in similar, and strongly agential, terms, with 75% nominating 'leadership' as being the only cause of Yemen's serious problems.[14] A further 6% said that leadership (or other agential factors such as 'political vision' or 'political will') was one of the causes, that is, they also believed that factors relating to either bad luck or the quality of the Yemeni people were important. Some GPC or government officials focused on natural resources and the quality of Yemen's citizens, but many of them later alluded to elite agency-based prerequisites to solving the problems. In total, therefore, 81% of participants nominated factors pertaining to the unwillingness of the country's leadership to confront the challenges as being the most important cause of the problems.[15] Structural restrictions were perceived to be tight in the spaces where the party elite operates, but the room for agency at the top was perceived to be high.

When discussing their own individual capacities to solve the problems they identified, perceptions again varied little across party lines: participants strongly felt they were too weak to influence the course of events because power is concentrated at the top and that, therefore, offering advice to the leadership was the most effective option available to them. While this response could be expected from the JMP, in fact, participants from the ruling party also underlined the helplessness of their own party to a considerable degree, as is demonstrated below. Several government ministers also noted that neither the GPC nor the government was able to take effective action against Yemen's problems. The opposition, on the other hand, believed that their inability to affect changes was due to the concentration of power in either the GPC or President Saleh.

Even though most participants perceived that decisive action was in their collective interests, they felt that their individual latitude for movement was negligible. There was a strong perception, however, that it was in the president's power to solve Yemen's problems to a considerable degree, if he would only mobilise the resources at his disposal towards this outcome. This was noted by participants from both sides, including individuals with direct access to Saleh.

For example, when asked what capacity his party had to solve Yemen's problems, a GPC member of parliament – the closest regime insider interviewed for this study – lamented: 'None, because of the mentality ... there is a lack of vision.' Other rumblings of discontent were made public through US diplomatic cables released by WikiLeaks:

> Largely unprecedented criticism of Saleh's leadership within the rarified circle of Saleh's closest advisors has increased in recent months, even including long-time Saleh loyalists such as Office of the Presidency aides [redacted], according to [redacted]. These names add to the growing chorus of Saleh loyalists that have shed their traditional aversion to disparaging the man they call 'The Boss'...[16]

Along similar lines, a senior member of the GPC commented: 'The GPC is not a party. It is a party for the leader ... only when there is political will anyone be able to get anything done.' When asked what his individual responsibility as a leader is to work towards solutions, he commented: 'there is only one leader, so don't ask me that.' A former cabinet member and member of the Majlis al-Shura[17] commented on the problems facing the country: 'It's corruption and ineffective government and after that it's the decline of water resources. These are all serious but temporary ... It's really the leadership, but how can I say it?' When asked about the most effective way to solve Yemen's problems, he said: 'Trust between the leader and the followers.' In other words, the president should trust the people around him enough to devolve some power to them. In his estimation, all responsibility ultimately lay with President Saleh. He said that his individual responsibility was only to 'advise the president'.

A member of the GPC's General Committee elaborated on this feeling of powerlessness further: initially he was uncomfortable using the term 'leadership' to describe the causes of Yemen's problems, and requested that the term 'political system' be used instead, even making certain that 'political system' replaced the word 'leadership' on the form. However, when he noted that the GPC had no power to solve any of Yemen's problems he stated that this was 'because the *political system* does not allow it'.

> Q: What is your responsibility as a leader in solving the problems facing Yemen?
> A: None.
> Q: Is it still your intention to try to work toward a solution or has the problem/s become too serious for you to have an impact?
> A: I've given up.

In another indication of the restriction of influence to a small group of insiders, a Yemeni diplomat with close links to the regime's leadership responded to the question of how he could be more effective as a leader, saying: 'by gaining the confidence of the [president's] family'. The implication was that if the inner circle does not trust a person, they lose access to President Saleh. Another diplomat with close access to the president commented similarly that the GPC cannot solve any of Yemen's problems because 'it's not as a party, it's people – some people in the party can make the difference by developing solutions and giving advice'. When asked if other countries might be more effective at solving Yemen's problem he answered: 'Yes – unless the leader takes the lead on reforms.'

A senior GPC technocrat commented that the main cause of Yemen's problems was 'the absence of governance, absence of the rule of law, paralysed institutions, [state] intervention in justice and the centralisation of power. The latter is the most important.'

> Q: What are the solutions to the problems?
> A: Crisis is inevitable. The only solution is complete system reform.
> Q: Which of the problems does your party have the ability to solve?
> A: None ... the party and government are paralysed because of the concentration of power.
> Q: What is your responsibility as a leader in solving the problem/s facing Yemen?
> A: Offering advice and suggesting solutions to decision makers.
> Q: How could you be more effective?
> A: If I wasn't receiving my salary from the government then I would be more effective.

These comments were made by a ranking figure within the ruling party, who was selected on the basis of access to President Saleh, and for having a public record of developmentally inclined actions. The survey results reveal that participants perceived their own structural constraints to be tight but believed there was wide latitude for agency at the top. However, it appears that they underestimated the structural constraints that President Saleh faced from within his inner circle, and the inability of that group to respond to change without rupturing.

CHAPTER SEVEN

Yemen and the 2011 Arab Uprisings

In early 2011 Middle Eastern politics took an unanticipated turn. The horrific image of a despairing young man setting himself on fire to protest at the injustice of the Tunisian regime articulated the sense of hopelessness that had become prevalent across the region. His death proved to be the catalyst for a wave of popular protest that swept through Tunisia and then Egypt, removing their presidents and putting the region's other leaders on alert. In Bahrain, Libya, Syria and Yemen there were major protests calling for their leaders to follow the Tunisian and Egyptian presidents into retirement. The initial results of these protests have varied and their long-term outcomes remain unpredictable, but the uprisings still signify one of the most important political changes in the region for decades. The 2011 protests have shown that, for the first time in a long time, political engagement is something that has a purpose for ordinary citizens. In the case of Egypt, it took just 18 days of concerted effort to end Hosni Mubarak's 30-year rule and the successful demands for change there have become a galvanising force across the region.

The trickle of protesters that took to the streets in Yemen following the departure of the Tunisian president turned into a flood within two months.[1] Despite this, the JMP was initially reluctant to become involved as a coalition and instead held 'festivals', during which its leaders talked about poverty and corruption but refrained from calling for Saleh's resignation or making comparisons with Tunisia. While the JMP did move to offer formal support to the protestors later, it stopped short of joining their calls for radical change to the system.

This underscores that the JMP and the street protesters are discrete entities with different agendas. It has always been part of the Yemeni political settlement that this elite opposition should remain open to dialogue with the ruling party; in this respect, the JMP differs markedly from the crowds in the street, who are less willing to negotiate. Importantly, both the JMP and the Gulf Cooperation Council transition initiative favour keeping political power in Yemen within the elite (broadly defined). Thus neither the official opposition nor Saudi Arabia stood for transition to a government that represented or involved the protesters thronging the streets of Sana'a, Ta'izz and elsewhere.

Saleh's attempts to contain the growing unrest were entirely familiar to anyone who had watched events unfold in Tunisia and Egypt. Many of the pro-government 'supporters' had military haircuts; the regime handed out chicken, rice and cash to people in Tahreer Square in Sana'a in a bid to win their support; and pay increases were offered to civil servants in return for their loyalty. Saleh also promised to deliver genuine political reforms and vowed – as he did in both 1999 and 2005 – not to contest the next presidential elections. Again not straying far from the responses of his regional counterparts, Saleh revived old pejoratives against those who had taken to the streets,[2] and claimed that the protests were the handiwork of America and Israel.[3]

Despite his efforts, Saleh's support began to unravel very publicly within the three most important pillars of political power in the country: the tribes, the religious elite and the military. On 17 February, Hussein al-Ahmar (the son of Sheikh Abdullah and half-brother of Hameed) announced that if the government continued to fight the protesters, he would bring 50,000 Hashid tribesmen to Sana'a to protect them. On the same day, the influential cleric Abdul-Majeed al-Zindani held a meeting at his home and read a prepared statement. His statement largely followed the government's official line about the protests but included the declaration that attacking peaceful demonstrators was *haram* (prohibited by Islam). During the questions from the audience that followed, Zindani went further, thanking al-Jazeera for its coverage of the uprisings in Tunisia and Egypt, and saying that if the president's relatives resigned from their military positions it would help to calm the situation.[4]

On 14 March, four Western journalists were expelled from the country. While they were not the first to be removed from Yemen – the government had been working to restrict access for journalists and researchers for at least 18 months – their removal was ominous. Four days later, snipers armed with Dragunov rifles occupied the buildings that overlook University Square (or 'Taghair' – Change — Square as it was called by protesters) in Sana'a and in a short and violent outburst, 52 peaceful protestors were killed and hundreds more were wounded. Some footage of the incident suggests that the snipers were particularly targeting those with hand-held cameras. Local sources that were in the area at the time said that ambulances were prevented from entering the streets surrounding the square, and that government hospitals were instructed not to assist the injured.[5]

Three days later, the internal cohesion of the Saleh regime ruptured spectacularly when Ali Muhsin publicly defected in protest against the massacre, and was followed by several other senior figures in the military. His defection effectively brought to an end the political settlement that had held the regime's inner circle together for more than 32 years. Despite this, some disbelieving Yemenis still suspected that the defections must have been part of a tactic to help the regime to maintain power, such was the level of public shock created by Muhsin's move.

As tensions built over the following days and weeks, it appeared that troops loyal to the newly competing factions of the regime (that is, Ali Muhsin's 1st Armoured Division and President Saleh's Republican Guard) were preparing for a violent confrontation. The two groups established opposing checkpoints throughout Sana'a and there was sporadic (although initially small-scale) fighting between them. Sources close to the Sanhan tribe reported that there was retaliation for these skirmishes within the tribe.[6]

Closed-door negotiations between President Saleh, Ali Muhsin and members of the JMP in late March and early April made little headway, with the main sticking point being whether President Saleh's sons, nephews and other members of the inner circle (including Ali Muhsin) would retain their military positions in the event of Saleh's resignation.[7] In April, the Gulf Cooperation Council (GCC) responded to the stalemate by proposing an initiative that was intended to coax Saleh from office, with the promise of immunity for him and his family. The GCC initiative allowed President Saleh to remain in power for 30 days after signing the agreement, after which power was to be transferred to a transitional national unity government comprised of existing political figures. Under this arrangement the transitional government would rule for 60 days, after which presidential elections would be held. The haste of this intended transition plan granted little space to the country's emerging political forces, such as those driving the protests, to forge the structures and alliances necessary to be competitive in an election. The initiative – over which Saleh prevaricated – illustrated the GCC member states' preference for a stable transition steered by familiar hands.

Confrontations between the supporters of the al-Ahmar family and President Saleh worsened in May, when Saleh loyalists shelled Sadiq al-Ahmar's house during the meeting of a mediation committee. One of the mediators was killed and others were seriously injured, from which point the situation descended into tit-for-tat violence between the two sides. The government tried to close off access to Sana'a to prevent more Hashid tribesmen from entering the city to support the al-Ahmars, while petrol became increasingly scarce and food prices increased.

On 3 June, an attempt was made on President Saleh's life. An explosion in the mosque on the presidential compound during Friday prayers killed a number of Republican Guardsmen and seriously wounded some of Yemen's most senior officials, including the prime minister, two of his deputies, the head of the Consultative Council, and the speaker of parliament. President Saleh was supposed to appear on television to show that he had survived the attack but instead gave only an audio address in which his breathing sounded strained. The following day he authorised the transition of power to the vice president and left the country for Saudi Arabia to seek medical treatment for the injuries that he sustained in the blast.

From this position, there appear to be three obvious scenarios for Yemen's short- to medium-term future: that Saleh stage an audacious return to Yemen; that he die or leave via a negotiated transition but the system he has created is not fundamentally altered; or that the regime is swept away. Saleh or his family could only maintain power with the continued support of the

Republican Guard (against possible confrontation from rival military factions and tribal irregulars) and the northern tribes, as well as the flow of money from external sources, most notably from Saudi Arabia, and by exercising control over Yemen's oil. Equally important under this scenario is the ability to at least partially freeze out Ali Muhsin and reconfigure the regime's inner and out circles without him.

The outbreak of civil war is a possibility under any scenario, particularly if the longstanding personal acrimony between the al-Ahmar family and President Saleh's family increases. Despite the obvious combustibility of the situation, there are some factors that may help to reduce the chances of a long-term civil war. Firstly, while Saleh's son commands the Republican Guard, many of the Guardsmen have family and tribal kinsmen in both Ali Muhsin's 1st Armoured Division and in the tribes that support the al-Ahmar family. The relatively narrow geographical and tribal origins of these three key groups could help to at least limit the potential for resorting to deadly force over an extended period. Secondly, although the availability of arms is often cited as a factor that increases the risk of civil war, it could also work the other way. Ordinary Yemenis are acutely aware that violence can spiral exponentially as a result of small miscalculations. The fact that the protesters were resolutely nonviolent despite the regime's violence against them was just one indication of how well this is understood. In tribal conflicts, for example, the goal is less to vanquish an opponent than to demonstrate the ability to apply symbolic force in defence of one's position and then to negotiate a solution in which both sides retain honour. While this tends to lay a foundation for theatrical brinkmanship in which the cost of miscalculation is both real and high, it also means that violent outbursts tend to be relatively short-lived. As of June 2011, the casualties caused by the fighting between the Ahmars and those loyal to Saleh were lower than one might expect, considering the amount of firepower used.

Yemen's modern history is full of short, sharp conflicts, but it is when outside powers have intervened, as in the 1962–1970 northern civil war – which became a proxy fight between Egypt and Saudi Arabia – that war has become most intractable. This observation provides all the more reason to worry about the deep involvement not just of Saudi Arabia but also the United States, with its focus on fighting al-Qaeda. Both players may be helping to set the stage for the regime's internal rivalries to explode – with dire consequences for the Yemeni people.

Why did Saleh take Yemen on such a disastrous course?

While the internal calculations of President Saleh are impossible to prove, many of his public statements suggest that, unlike the participants surveyed for this study, he believed Yemen's challenges were minor and temporary. For example, in an interview with Abu Dhabi Television in January 2010, he commented that the problems in the south (that is, the grassroots secessionist movement) had been heavily exaggerated and were really just a matter of 'dozens or hundreds' of people.[8] Likewise, in an interview with Dubai Sports in December 2009, Saleh reassured his interviewer that Yemen's Gulf Soccer Tournament would go ahead as scheduled in November 2010, and would not be affected by the war in Sa'da because 'the war is about 600 kilometres away'.[9] It appears that President Saleh's apparent lack of great concern derived from his confidence in three factors.

First among these reasons was his proven ability to extract funds from Yemen's neighbours, particularly Saudi Arabia. Access to this funding meant that President Saleh believed that he could probably maintain power even if the threats facing ordinary citizens (particularly household food insecurity) continued to worsen. As discussed above, in 2009 Yemen received $2.2 billion in untied money from Saudi Arabia and a further $700 million from the UAE, making the total (known) amount around two-thirds of what Yemen earned from oil exports when revenues peaked in 2008.[10] In 2010, Saudi Arabia contributed at least $1bn in untied funding, though most estimates also put this figure closer to $2bn. This does not include the money that Saudi Arabia pays directly to Yemen's tribes. Libya also contributed $500m in a fixed deposit to the Yemeni Central Bank in 2010.

There is money to be made from crisis, just as there is leverage to be gained when the state over which you preside is seen to pose a threat to regional and international security. External actors have, therefore, helped to frustrate the emergence of a political alternative by facilitating the regime's short-term rent-seeking behaviour and reducing its incentives to risk its survival in the short term by finding longer-term solutions that would improve the livelihoods of its citizens.

However, President Saleh's beliefs about his personal importance to internal Saudi politics also apparently distorted the accuracy of his threat perceptions. An article by Hussein Leswaas in November 2010, a journalist widely known within Yemen to write pieces that have been intentionally leaked by the palace, suggested this possibility. The article, 'The Role of the President in the Factional Conflict in Saudi Arabia', argued that President Saleh has played a pivotal role in mediating the dispute between King Abdullah and other members of the Saudi royal family, noting that: 'the president has played key roles in restructuring alignments within the two blocs'.[11] Media articles about the relationship between Yemen and Saudi Arabia are considered highly sensitive by the Yemeni regime and it is most unlikely that an article of this nature, and with this level of detail about internal Saudi politics, would have been printed without permission at the highest level. This suggests that President Saleh may have believed that he was indispensible to Saudi Arabia and that his leverage within the kingdom – and by extension, his ability to continue to access funds – was guaranteed. In this respect, he miscalculated: a 2009 cable from the American Embassy in Riyadh notes, for example: 'We have seen no evidence that the King has any particular regard for Saleh beyond exasperation that borders on disgust.'[12] Saudi support for the GCC transition agreement made abundantly clear the kingdom's belief that Saleh had become expendable.

Secondly, President Saleh thrived in a volatile environment. The fewer rules and institutions there are, the wider his room for manoeuvre, and the more opportunities to create rivalries among opponents. For those in the upper echelons of the Yemeni regime, the reproduction of power and wealth has been facilitated by managed crisis, and so what outsiders typically see as instability has looked rather different to the inner circle. This is because of the potential that crisis offers for generating further rents, whether through international grants, foreign security assistance (which can be deployed against domestic political opponents), or through the low levels of law and order that facilitate smuggling and other criminal activity. From this perspective, formalised rational–legal constraints to the regime's ability to generate rents pose a greater short-term threat to its interests than the possibility of violent conflict, an economic crash or famine. Violent conflict was not necessarily seen to pose as great a threat to the regime as outsiders, particularly in the West, believed. In fact, crisis can create opportunities.

Finally, President Saleh believed that there were no alternative political power centres (progressive or otherwise, formal or otherwise) that could seize power from him. Saleh has fostered deeply entrenched fears of chaos among an already vulnerable, divided and under-educated population. The political forces

that had emerged prior to 2011, such as the southern secessionist movement, the al-Houthis, AQAP and Hameed al-Ahmar's
Preparatory Committee for National Dialogue had all failed to
convince the Yemeni public that they could lead the country
in President Saleh's stead. Until Mubarak's departure radically altered the perception of human agency in Arab national
politics, the Yemeni public and the political party elite alike
appeared to believe that, for all of its faults, the leadership of
President Saleh was still not the worst available option.

While members of the opposition still drew at least some
benefit from the political status quo, they had been justifiably
wary of provoking too harsh a response from the regime. They
realised that opting out of the system by demanding genuine
reform – that is, reform that targeted the president and his
inner circle – risked marginalisation. They may have seen the
system as flawed, but many still believed that its likely alternative was chaos. Political demands that threatened the regime,
and thus the system itself, were generally seen as counterproductive.[13] The survey conducted for the Developmental
Leadership Program revealed that even in late 2010 most of
Yemen's political party elite still saw President Saleh as being
central to any process of 'safe' change. Even though the opposition has long referred to regime change, they did not take
the risk of substantively challenging the president, whom they
still appeared to consider as the father of the nation, or at least
the person most likely to deliver them with individual benefits
through the patronage system.

What did most observers know that Saleh did not?

Saleh's calculations that he could prevail despite the vulnerability of ordinary citizens were also seriously flawed. The
interviewees' collective belief that Yemen faced a serious crisis
suggests that Saleh's preference for tone-deaf 'yes' men over

the political and technocratic advisers that he once favoured left him without a nuanced understanding of the changes under way in Yemeni society. In seeking to cement a power-hierarchy that protected the political settlement of his inner circle, he had little agility to deal with scenarios that did not fit within his narrow model of people's expected behaviours. When people deviated from that model, his institutions were poorly equipped to adapt. In failing to protect feedback mechanisms that deliver society's reaction to the behaviour of the state in a regular, safe and nonviolent manner – whether through fair elections, the media, opinion polls or legal demonstrations – he left his regime vulnerable to demonstrations, riots, insurgency and revolution.

Yemen faces a period of significant turmoil. The country's structural problems are enormous – depleting oil and water reserves, an increasingly food-insecure population, a bloated and inefficient military and civil service and costly subsidies on petroleum products. It is likely that the measures needed to tackle these problems will prove so unpopular that any government willing to implement them would almost certainly undermine their longer-term political aspirations. This means that any leader with such aspirations is likely to continue to resist implementing the deep reforms that Yemen needs to undertake to remain a viable state.

Why Yemen hasn't helped itself: three collective-action problems

The failure to alter the country's ruinous course is partly attributable to collective-action problems within the three key groups of Yemeni elites that might be expected to catalyse change. These barriers can be seen in the system of patronage that includes almost all of the country's politically relevant elites, in the political settlement that holds the members of the

JMP together in coalition, and finally in the political settlement that maintained the regime's inner circle.

In the case of the patronage system, the high level of inclusiveness has resulted in a diversity of opinion and motivation that militates against group cohesion. This makes it very difficult for elites to negotiate changes to the status quo, if that even was their goal. The common denominator in this group – willingly or otherwise – is complicity in the rent-seeking behaviour of the state, and dissent is thus focused on the distribution of rents and favours rather than on issues of development. Action that may be collectively rational for the longer-term survival of the group, such as an end to their reliance on short-term rent-seeking, is individually irrational and is thus stifled.

Members of the JMP have also been constrained by a collective-action problem: ideologically and historically, they have little in common with each other; rather, they have been held together by the desire to protect themselves and occasionally to extract greater concessions, from the regime. The coalition's internal settlement is structured around the lowest common denominator which, while being an ineffectual basis for achieving developmental outcomes, has achieved the members' common aims of survival in an authoritarian environment. To remain united the members of the JMP cannot admit that Islah is the most politically powerful and relevant member of the group, lest the others appear irrelevant, and so each member has the authority to veto any group decision. The veto has helped to maintain the myth of equality but has also enforced a bland uniformity on the coalition and an unwillingness to test new ideas or strategies. The irony of this situation is that, in trying to enforce collective rationality over individual rationality, the individual parties have been weakened to such a degree that their whole is less than the sum of its parts.

The possibility of agency-driven change has always been greatest within the regime's inner circle which, by contrast, is a highly exclusive group. Its collective-action problem has, therefore, had the most significant impact on the lack of developmental reform within the country. Despite the clear advantages of incumbency, President Saleh was structurally constrained by the expectations of his inner circle, none of whom has displayed characteristics to suggest that they are developmentally inclined. To implement developmental reforms, President Saleh would have needed to upend the system of privilege that allowed the inner circle's predation to continue, and in doing so he would have almost certainly encountered serious resistance. The inner circle, therefore, created a structure that reinforced their agential disinclination for reform. President Saleh exercised almost absolute control when it came to maintaining the status quo that benefited his inner circle, but was quite constrained in his ability to alter their political settlement. Many of the constraints that bound Saleh are likely to bind his successors. This raises questions for how Western donors can target anti-developmental settlements that are grounded in agential preference, which are discussed shortly.

The role of external policy
i) The security lens
Like the Pakistani leadership, Yemen's could be described as negotiating 'with its allies and friends by pointing a gun to its own head'.[1] The Yemeni regime has been acutely aware of the chaos that the international community believes could result from its demise and has wielded this threat deftly against calls for political and/or economic reforms. As long as the Yemeni threat to international security remains the prism through which all other policy is seen, the Yemeni regime will have the upper hand in deferring the difficult process of reform.

The West and Yemen's neighbours have both been clear at times that they were willing to use exceptional measures to support the Saleh regime against collapse. For example, US Secretary of State Hillary Clinton stated to the first Friends of Yemen meeting in January 2010: 'Some might ask, given the past history, why we should feel compelled to offer more assistance to Yemen. The answer is that we cannot afford inaction.'[2] This external view of Yemen has provided the regime with considerable leverage (real and perceived) against the international community. It has also provided disincentives for the regime to shift its rent-seeking business model to one that nurtures the economy or bargains with its citizens for its legitimacy. While this remains so, it will be less politically costly for the regime to bargain with the international community for support than to restructure Yemen's collusive, and often predatory, political settlements.

Conscious of the security threat Yemen wields, President Barack Obama responded to the 18 March massacre by saying: 'those responsible for today's violence must be held accountable',[3] thereby carefully avoiding the thorny issue of President Saleh's responsibility. Secretary Gates also tried to avoid commenting on the behaviour of America's ally when he noted: 'I don't think it's my place to talk about internal affairs in Yemen.' Gates later elaborated when asked by a journalist how dangerous a post-Saleh Yemen was to the United States. His answer articulated the vain hope that President Saleh remained the man to prevent al-Qaeda from gaining ground in Yemen: 'We've had counter-terrorism cooperation with President Saleh and the Yemeni security services ... So if that government collapses, or is replaced by one who is dramatically more weak, then I think we'd face some additional challenges out of Yemen, there's no question about it.'[4]

ii) Perverse incentives

The impediments to change clearly underline the importance of exogenous factors in the maintenance of Yemen's dysfunctional political settlements. Yemen poses a security threat to its neighbours and to the international community, which has increased the willingness of external actors to guarantee the financial survival of the Saleh regime despite its inability or unwillingness to nurture the domestic economy for the same purpose. This has created a series of perverse incentives for President Saleh, as experience has taught him that foreign governments will offer more money with fewer strings attached if the threat posed by Yemeni militancy is credible.

President Saleh's penchant for releasing militant jihadis from prison in times of crisis underlines this point. The release of the 70 al-Qaeda suspects in March 2011 was not an isolated incident; it was part of a pattern of releases and pardons over which Saleh has presided, including that of Jamal al-Badawi, the convicted architect of the USS *Cole* bombing. In 2007, Saleh also pardoned Fahd al-Quso for his role in the *Cole* attack. In 2010, al-Quso re-emerged in an AQAP video, apparently unrepentant, and threatening to again attack US interests. One might reasonably argue that releasing members of AQAP is counterintuitive; after all, the group has actively threatened President Saleh's leadership and members of his security services. Saleh has even risked his domestic credibility by permitting the US to conduct airstrikes against AQAP on Yemeni territory. Under what circumstances, therefore, could releasing members of AQAP be to his advantage? The answer is that Saleh built his power on an informal system that runs on crisis, and al-Qaeda are agents of crisis. The presence of al-Qaeda in Yemen makes it far more likely that the West will continue to look at the country through a counter-terrorism prism at the exclusion of other important issues. It also increases the probability that the West will argue for stability and orderliness rather than for dramatic change. Deputy Assistant US Secretary of Defense for Special Operations and Combating Terrorism Garry Reid commented in March 2011 that President Saleh's government was 'the best partner we're going to have ... and hopefully it will survive because I certainly would hate to start over again in what we've tried to build'.[5]

However, the assumption that Saleh had been the 'best partner we're going to have' against AQAP is open to dispute, and one source close to President Saleh noted in late 2010 that his strategy had in fact been to 'sell al-Qaeda to the highest bidder' as a means of maintaining relevance.[6] By sanctioning the release of prisoners, Saleh appeared to be trying to insure himself against becoming obsolete. For a man who ruled by creating chaos and confusion among those who might challenge him, releasing people who can who can graphically illustrate just how dangerous Yemen is helped to reduce the probability of genuine change.

iii) Policy disconnections

The regime's inner circle (the informal state) has dominated political decision-making and resource allocation but it is the government (the formal state) that Western donors have expected to deliver systemic changes in exchange for greater support. However, Yemen's political volatility and lack of economic growth has been as much a matter of choice as it is a matter of structural capacity, which puts donors in an awkward position. Dealing with matters of agency and elite self-interest is outside the traditional purview of donors, who work with more tangible issues of capacity, hoping to mould developmentally progressive leaders by creating the right tools for them to do their work. Often, and in the case of Yemen, this puts the cart before the horse. It also encourages expensive palliative measures – propping up an ill-adapted formal shell – rather than the processes that might eventually develop cures. Technical reforms to Yemen's government institutions are unlikely to have a significant impact unless there is also a sea change in the politics that determines where power is located. This will be even more important as the country moves to a post-Saleh era. The longer-term developments that are likely to enable this include the higher education of its citizens (particularly at tertiary levels where critical thought is a focus), and the evolution of a more cooperative relationship between the political and the economic elites.

The disconnection between problems and solutions can also be seen at the more local level of donor interventions, in which aggrieved tribal communities are prioritised at the expense of the poorest parts of the country and the traditional commercial centres. Through its Community Livelihoods Project for Yemen, USAID is targeting development assistance at the areas that AQAP has established a presence, including 'Amraan, al-Jawf, Marib, Shabwa, Abyan, Al-Dhala'e, Lahj and Aden.[7] However, while these parts of the country are certainly vulnerable, they are not necessarily the *most* vulnerable, particularly if levels of household food security are used as an indicator.[8] The logic of targeting these eight governorates stems instead from the fact that most serious external security concerns are based there.[9] With the exception of Aden, these parts of Yemen traditionally produce little and are, therefore, unlikely to drive national economic growth in the short term.[10] If donor engagement is to move from palliatives to corrective measures then this prioritisation may be counterproductive.

Furthermore, if the nature and presence of the government is part of problem that AQAP is preying on in these areas, then reinvigorating that 'presence and legitimacy' is not necessarily the solution and could even exacerbate the problem.[11] Finally, by prioritising these governorates for development assistance, the livelihoods programme risks tacitly incentivising both militancy and rent-seeking without necessarily addressing the root causes of AQAP's traction. Just as importantly, it risks overlooking the areas from which economic regeneration may be more likely to emerge in the longer term: the parts of the country that have a robust history of pragmatic commerce, entrepreneurship, high levels of education, and of spreading wealth well beyond their local communities through trade, particularly around the governorate of Ta'izz.

The governorate of Ta'izz (along with the neighbouring governorate of Ibb) constitutes the most populous and fertile part of Yemen. Having long been considered the 'bread basket of Yemen' for its relative abundance of productive land, Ta'izz is the country's most important commercial and intellectual centre, and is home to the country's traditional merchant class. Within Yemen, people from Ta'izz have a reputation for being the best educated, and the area prides itself on the quality of schooling available. One finds people from Ta'izz in every part of the country; teaching in schools, running small businesses, working in government offices and in the lower echelons of the military. While the author is not aware of any reliable statistical data on how much is produced in Ta'izz compared to the rest of the country, a quick visit to the region is enough to attest to the priority that is attached to industry, production, trade and education compared with the northern highlands area that surrounds Sana'a. A longer-term and less securitised view of development aid to Yemen would almost certainly place a greater emphasis on encouraging the productive capacity of areas like Ta'izz, the carryover benefits of which are likely to be greater than the narrow approach currently in play.

Difficult choices

In most conversations about appropriate strategies for Western donors in Yemen over the past few years, the term 'quick runs on the board' (or similar variations thereof) has been invoked, for which there is usually a security imperative: the need to quickly stabilise an area that is vulnerable to violence or militancy.[12] While this is understandable in the prevailing climate, the focus on quick-impact projects reinforces two misconceptions. Firstly, that political instability is a function of *government* ineffectiveness and can therefore be turned around by making the government more effective irrespective of the shadow state; and, secondly, that political instability can (and should) be prevented by these projects. This focus masks the fact that what Yemen needs – and has long needed – more than 'stability' is change.

Though the changes that swept the Arab world in 2011 will take many years to fully manifest themselves, it is clear that Western policies towards the region – particularly the support for unpopular regimes – have not engendered greater stability. As the search begins for new strategies to facilitate stable political settlements in Middle Eastern states, policymakers will face several dilemmas.

Firstly, given that a lasting solution to security threats requires fundamental change rather than near-constant crisis suppression and stabilisation, is there any way to avoid a trade-off between less short-term security and greater long-term security? At a superficial level, such a trade-off seems unavoidable but the dilemma may be largely one of risk perception and the need to be seen to act decisively. The 2011 uprisings across the region appear to testify against the notion that short-term security can be purchased at the expense of a state's longer-term development and self determination. A critical question, therefore, becomes whether there is a way to avoid a *perceived* trade-off between less short-term security and more long-term security in front of a domestic audience? In other words, can a Western audience perceive the risks associated with political instability in the Middle East to be potentially beneficial for building more stable polities in the future and, moreover, something over which its elected officials can exercise little real positive influence in the short-term? US Secretary of State Hillary Clinton and others have repeatedly stressed their concerns that a power vaccuum or a civil war in Yemen may play into al-Qaeda's hands.

Secondly, what constraints does Saudi Arabia impose? The West cannot realistically match the level of financial assistance that Yemen's neighbours can provide, and Saudi Arabia has clearly demonstrated its ability to bankroll the Yemeni regime to a very significant degree. Saudi Arabia has its own interests and motivations in Yemen and is not shy in pursuing them. Therefore, one of the most important constraints facing Western objectives in Yemen is the red lines that are drawn by the kingdom. Saudi Arabia does not want to see state collapse in Yemen but neither does it wish to see the emergence of a genuinely democratic and inclusive political settlement that could threaten its own internal political arrangements. The kingdom's willingness to send troops into Bahrain to quell the March 2011 uprising in Manama is a strong indicator of the political fault lines that it perceives at home, and of the influence that it believes its neighbours can have over its domestic affairs. Saudi Arabia's overriding preference for 'stability' in Yemen means the maintenance of a weak and dependent Yemen and it will not embrace a radically new political order emerging in its neighbour. Political change in Yemen will need to be seen through the prism of what is acceptable to Saudi Arabia, and though what the kingdom is willing and able to do to enforce its preferences. Whatever the West's engagement with Yemen is in the future, Saudi Arabia will to a large extent set the perameteres of the possible.

Thirdly, there is the question of how to engage with informal institutions and the powerful shadow elite. At present, Western governments and donor agencies have almost no access to the regime's inner circle, and therefore, almost no communication with the shadow state that makes the important decisions. Opening these lines of communication needs to be a priority, with a view to discussing the longer-term incentives for this group to work towards a post-rentier economy and foster national economic growth. While the shadow elite do not hold official political positions, many (if not most) of them are deeply involved in the national economy. They work as the local agents for international energy companies, they own security companies that are hired to protect foreign embassies and companies, and they own companies that trade internationally. They might, therefore, be accessed through their business positions rather than their through their informal political positions. Such engagement is a necessary (but by no means sufficient) condition for gaining any credibility or influence with the country's real decision-makers.

Finally, what can be done to fix the problem of perverse incentives? The Yemeni regime has benefited from being able to bargain with the international community as a supplier of a multi-faceted threat to international security. The West and the GCC have legitimised this approach by explicitly supporting the regime on this basis. Until the lopsided approach to the country's leadership is altered by external actors, the leadership's incentives to stifle domestic economic development and keep the country's insurgencies smouldering are likely to endure. This dilemma is all the greater when one considers that Saudi Arabia holds many of the cards. This underlines the importance of taking a longer-term approach in which the goal is to facilitate – or, importantly, not to inhibit – the space that is available to local actors seeking to bargain with the leadership.

With regard to economic development, the obstacles facing investors in Yemen are constructed (or at least permitted) by the regime to a significant degree and could be diminished if it became in the collective self-interest of the leadership to do so. Yemen is a particularly risky place to invest capital because of its poor rule of law, and entrenched rent-seeking and investors have largely declined to put their money into the country for these reasons. The lack of private investment has furthered the centralisation of wealth and power in the regime's hands. Bearing in mind the level of risk facing investors, donors might look to facilitate a shift in the balance of economic power towards society, perhaps by offering venture capital insurance programmes for local private investors who are willing to risk investing in Yemeni projects. Stimulating economic development in this manner is a long-term process, but it could be part of a package aimed to develop the greater interdependence of Yemen's merchants with Yemen's political leadership. Neopatrimonialism is not inherently anti-developmental; the level of political and economic centralisation found in Yemen could facilitate greater economic growth if the regime chose to favour that outcome. The leadership could choose to reduce the political hurdles that currently impede investors – such as the insistence that they partner with members of the inner circle, or the unwritten requirement that they evade taxation in order to be competitive – in exchange for their ability to deliver economic growth.

The real instability within Yemen is that which affects its vulnerable citizens. What has worked for the Yemeni regime has not worked for its citizens, and the international community needs to decide what it hopes to stabilise through its interventions: the regime or its citizens. In so doing, it should keep in mind that support for the former has not brought stability.

NOTES

Introduction

1   It is beyond the purposes of this book to dissect the various meanings of the term 'food security', but the definition used here is drawn from the Food and Agriculture Organization of the United Nations World Food Summit in 1996: 'all people, at all times, have physical and economic access to sufficient, safe and nutritious food to meet their dietary needs and food preferences for an active and healthy life'. This is the definition that is used in the World Food Programme, *Comprehensive Food Security Survey: Republic of Yemen*, March 2010, p. 14, which found that 31.5% of Yemenis are food-insecure.

2   The release was reported on Islah's *Suhail* satellite channel, and was believed by some within Yemen to have been fabricated by Islah. It was confirmed, however, by a security source who attended the Political Security Organisation (PSO) prison in Sana'a shortly after the release, and confirmed by a ranking GPC official. Personal communications, March 2011.

3   Robert D Burrowes, 'The Famous Forty and their Companions: North Yemen's First-Generation Modernists and Educational Emigrants', *Middle East Journal*, vol. 59 no. 1, 2005, pp. 81–97.

4   For further discussion of political settlements, see Thomas Parks and William Cole, 'Political Settlements: Implications for International Development Policy and Practice', Occasional Paper No. 02, 2010, *The Asia Foundation*, http://www.asiafoundation.org/resources/pdfs/PoliticalSettlementsFINAL.pdf; Jonathan Di John and James Putzel, 'Political Settlements' Issues Paper, *Governance and Social Development Resource Centre*, June 2009. http://www.gsdrc.org/docs/open/EIRS7.pdf .

5   Victoria Clark, *Yemen: Dancing on the Heads of Snakes* (New Haven, CT and London: Yale University Press, 2010), p. 139.

6   See Edward Laws, 'The "Revolutionary Settlement" in 17th Century England: Deploying a Political Settlements Analysis', *Developmental Leadership Program*, Background Paper 9, November 2010, for a discussion of the process by which the political settlement was forged in seventeenth-century England. For a more general

discussion of political settlements, see Thomas Parks and William Cole, 'Political Settlements'. See also Charles Tilly, 'War Making and State Making as Organized Crime', in P. Evans, D. Rueschemeyer and T. Skocpol (eds), *Bringing the State Back In* (Cambridge: Cambridge University Press, 1985).

7 Robert Jackson, *Quasi-States: Sovereignty, International Relations and the Third World* (Cambridge: Cambridge University Press, 1990).

8 Eva Bellin, 'Coercive Institutions and Coercive Leaders' in M. Pripstein Posusney and M. Penner Angrist,(eds), *Authoritarianism in the Middle East: Regimes and Resistance* (Boulder, CO: Lynne Rienner Publishers, 2005), pp. 21–41.

9 Sam Perlo-Freeman, 'Arms Transfers to the Middle East', *SIPRI Background Paper*, July 2009, http://www.unidir. org/pdf/activites/pdf3-act465.pdf.

10 Barak Barfi, 'Yemen on the Brink? The Resurgence of al Qaeda in Yemen', *New America Foundation, Counterterrorism Strategy Initiative Policy Paper*, January 2010; Christopher Boucek, 'Yemen: Avoiding a Downward Spiral', *Carnegie Endowment for International Peace*, September 2009, http://carnegieendowment.org/ files/yemen_downward_spiral.pdf; Stephen Day. 'The Political Challenge of Yemen's Southern Movement', *Carnegie Endowment for International Peace*, Middle March 2010, http:// carnegieendowment.org/files/yemen_ south_movement.pdf; Andrew M. Exum and Richard Fontaine, 'On the Knife's Edge: Yemen's Instability and the Threat to American Interests', Policy Brief, *Center for a New American Security*, November 2009; Ginny Hill, 'Yemen: Fear of Failure', *Chatham House Briefing Paper*, November 2008, http://www.chathamhouse. org.uk/files/12576_bp1108yemen. pdf; Gregory D. Johnsen 'Welcome to Qaedastan', *Foreign Policy*, January/ February 2010; Sarah Phillips, 'What Comes Next in Yemen: Al-Qaeda, the Tribes and State-Building', Carnegie Endowment for International Peace, March 2010; International Crisis Group, 'Yemen: Defusing the Saada Time Bomb', Middle East Report, no. 86, 27 May 2009, http://www. crisisgroup.org/~/media/Files/ Middle East North Africa/Iran Gulf/ Yemen/086 Yemen Defusing the Saada Time Bomb.ashx; Neil MacDonald and Rana Khalil, 'Report of the Assessment towards a "Whole of EU" Approach to State Building in Yemen: Addressing Fragility to Prevent State Failure', July 2009.

11 Adrian Leftwich, 'Beyond Institutions: Rethinking the Role of Leaders, Elites and Coalitions in the Institutional Formation of Developmental States and Strategies', *Forum for Development Studies*, vol. 37, no. 1, 2010, pp. 93–111.

12 The field research commenced just one month after the attempted bombing of Flight 253 to Detroit (Christmas Day 2009) was traced to al-Qaeda in Yemen (al-Qaeda in the Arabian Peninsula, or AQAP). This attack closely followed the US-assisted airstrikes against al-Qaeda members in Yemen, which intensified suspicions about foreigners and foreign governments in Yemen, and contributed to the belief that a US military invasion might be imminent.

13 The Developmental Leadership Program (DLP) is a multi-stakeholder initiative, supported by the Australian Government that examines the role

of human agency in processes of development. For more information about the program see: http://www.dlprog.org.

14 The GPC Permanent Committee consists of 1,300 members, but the vast majority of members have little political relevance. Those who are involved in setting the direction for the party number around 300, and include the 229 members of parliament (which includes the 33 cabinet members), the members of the General Committee (which usually varies between 30 and 33), some members of the Majlis al-Shura, and some heads of government sectors and departments. Therefore, of this 300, about 200 would at least fit into the first category of being developmentally inclined, about 150 would fit into the second, and around 75 belong in the third category. The JMP sample was divided into 12 Islah, six YSP, three Nasserist, five Ba'ath and three Hizb al-Haqq members. These participants were members of parliament and members of the leadership of these parties. In some instances the selection was made by the relevant party. Islah, Ba'ath, al-Haqq and the Nasserites assigned their representatives. The YSP assigned some of their representatives and others were encountered in meetings. The GPC was less willing to provide the research team with such lists, so participants were selected on the basis of their participation in developing policy (those who had been vocal in proposing policies in the past or who have access to the power centres that formulate policy). These elites are some of the best-educated and – for those in the GPC – the best positioned to help implement the technical solutions that

the president Saleh continues to call for in his rhetoric.

15 Direct access to the regime's inner circle is very restricted, and it was not possible to interview them directly; the formal political party elite's interactions with the regime have been used to help infer the perceptions within the regime's inner circle.

16 Adrian Leftwich, 'Beyond Institutions', p. 94.

17 Robert H. Bates, *When Things Fell Apart: State Failure in Late-Century Africa* (Cambridge: Cambridge University Press, 2009).

18 *Ibid.*, p.5.

19 Charles Tilly, 'War Making and State Making as Organized Crime', in P. Evans, D. Rueschemeyer and T. Skocpol (eds), *Bringing the State Back In*.

20 Robert H. Bates, *Violence and Prosperity: The Political Economy of Development* (New York: W.W. Norton, 2001), p. 85.

21 Robert H. Bates, *When Things Fell Apart: State Failure in Late-Century Africa*, p. 17. Bates notes that the creation of order rests upon three conditions: that the rate of taxation is appropriate (that is not so high that the citizens will not pay and not so low that the specialist will feel short-changed); that the rewards available to the specialist if it turns to predation are not too high; and that the specialist is not so greedy, impatient or insecure that it elects to discount its future earnings too heavily in order to benefit in the short term.

22 Robert H. Bates, *Violence and Prosperity: The Political Economy of Development*, pp. 86–7.

23 *Ibid.*, p. 66.

24 *Ibid.*

25 J. Scott, 'Modes of Power and the Re-conceptualization of Elites', in M. Savage and K. Williams (eds),

Remembering Elites (Oxford: Blackwell, 2008), p. 33, Cited in Adrian Leftwich, 'Beyond Institutions', p. 104.

26 With few exceptions, business elites are members of one (or more) of these other three groups.

Chapter One

1 The Republic of Yemen was established in 1990 when the 'northern' Yemen Arab Republic and the 'southern' People's Democratic Republic of Yemen unified. The two sides fought a civil war in 1994. The post-war period established the military dominance of the northern-based regime at the expense of southern elites but it did not help to forge an effective framework of institutional power. There has been no political settlement forged between northern and southern elites that is acceptable to both sides. For more on the southern movement see Stephen Day, 'The Political Challenge of Yemen's Southern Movement', Carnegie Endowment for International Peace, March 2010, http://carnegieendowment.org/files/yemen_south_movement.pdf.

2 It is based on diverse and loosely connected threads of discontent and its lack of leadership means that there is not a consistent front for the regime to engage with. This lack of leadership is the movement's greatest strength and its biggest weakness. Its members and sympathisers are easier to divide and less strategically coherent, but they are also much harder to co-opt – something that is of considerable benefit when competing with the standard playbook of the Saleh regime.

3 Former Prime Minister Haidar al-Attas is by far the most relevant member of the southern movement's external leadership. His involvement began at the outset of the protests in July 2007, when he gave an explosive interview stating that it was possible that Yemen could break apart into 'more than two' countries – implying that one of these 'countries' would be Hadhramaut. Attas is a native Hadhrami living in exile in Saudi Arabia and it seems unlikely that he would have made such a statement without prior clearance from his Saudi patrons, who do not take lightly the possibility of unwanted political clashes with their neighbours. Attas' behaviour has been widely viewed within Yemen as an indication of tacit support for Hadhrami secession from some elements within the Saudi regime. He is careful not to make his statements from within Saudi Arabia (instead he travels to the Emirates, Cairo or London) but his ongoing residence within Saudi Arabia has not been questioned by the Saudi regime.

4 International Crisis Group, 'Yemen: Defusing the Saada Time Bomb', Middle East Report, No. 86, 27 May 2009, http://www.crisisgroup.org/~/media/Files/Middle East North Africa/Iran Gulf/Yemen/086 Yemen Defusing the Saada Time Bomb.ashx.; Christopher Boucek 'War in Saada: From Local Insurrection to National Challenge', Carnegie Endowment for International Peace, May 2010, http://

www.carnegieendowment.org/files/ war_in_saada.pdf; Barak A. Salmoni, Bryce Loidolt and Madeleine Wells, 'Regime and Periphery in Northern Yemen: The Huthi Phenomenon', *RAND Corporation*, 2010, http://www. rand.org/pubs/monographs/2010/ RAND_MG962.sum.pdf.

5   The actual level of Iranian involvement is certainly overstated by Yemeni regime, but is difficult to ascertain with any clarity. The International Crisis Group (ICG) quotes a Western diplomat who puts it well: 'there is no clear evidence of Iranian involvement but small signs of a role by Iranian charitable organisations. Overall, however, the conflict appears chiefly fuelled by internal grievances.' ICG, 'Yemen: Defusing the Saada Time Bomb' p. 12.

6   This paragraph borrows from Sarah Phillips, 'Cracks in the Yemeni System', Middle East Report, 28 July 2005, http://www.merip.org/mero/ mero072805.

7   US Secretary of Defense Robert Gates, cited in Laura Kasinof and Robert F. Worth, 'Yemen's Leader Defiant Amid Protests and Defections', *New York Times*, 22 March 2011.

8   Al-Qaeda in the Arabian Peninsula, *Sada al-Malahim*, Volume 10, August 2009 (in Arabic).

9   Al-Qaeda in the Arabian Peninsula, *Sada al-Malahim*, Volume 8, March 2009 (in Arabic); Alistair Harris, 'Instrumentalizing Grievances: Al-Qaeda in the Arabian Peninsula', in Christopher Boucek and Marina Ottaway (eds), *Yemen on the Brink* (Washington DC: Carnegie Endowment for International Peace, 2010), p. 36.

10   Cited in Jeffrey Fleishman, 'Yemen President's Ouster May Deal U.S. Huge Setbacks', *LA Times*, 23 March 2011, http://www.latimes.com/ news/nationworld/world/la-fg-yemen-dangers-20110323,0,3343598. story?track=rss.

11   Cited in Erik Stier, 'Will Yemen Protests Boost Al Qaeda?', *Christian Science Monitor*, 25 March 2011, http://www.csmonitor.com/ World/Middle-East/2011/0325/ Will-Yemen-protests-boost-Al-Qaeda.

12   Ragui Assad et al., *'Youth Exclusion in Yemen: Tackling the Twin Deficits of Human Development and Natural Resources'*, Dubai School of Government, November 2009, p. 10.

13   World Food Programme, *Comprehensive Food Security Survey: Republic of Yemen*, March 2010, p.14.

14   Food and Agriculture Organization of the United Nations, 'FAO Food Price Index', 3 February 2011. http:// www.fao.org/worldfoodsituation/ FoodPricesIndex/en/.

15   Omar Naje, 'Yemen's Capital "will Run Out of Water by 2025"', *Science and Development Network*, 22 October 2010, http://www.scidev.net/en/ news/yemen-s-capital-will-run-out-of-water-by-2025-.html. However, predictions of this nature have been made for some time, see for example Christopher Ward, 'Yemen's Water Crisis', British Yemeni Society, July 2001, http://www.al-bab.com/bys/ articles/ward01.htm, which argues that 'In the Sana'a basin … Groundwater is expected to be pumped dry in the Sana'a basin within the next decade.'

16   Yemen consumes a considerable portion of the oil that it produces and so 'oil subsistence' refers to the point at which it is no longer producing enough oil to service even its domestic needs.

17 Economist Intelligence Unit, *Country Report: Yemen*, January 2010.

18 World Bank, *Yemen Economic Quarterly Review*, Summer 2010, p. 2. Higher international oil prices have made some previously decommissioned oil fields profitable again, but it is not possible to confidently predict the possibility of new oil fields coming online because this is dependent on several variables, including whether new discoveries are made, the ability of oil companies to raise the funding to extract the oil, and the international price of oil. Some within the oil industry remain confident that new discoveries are still likely, but the minimum time from discovery to production has thus far been four years.

19 Risk Watch, 'Yemeni Parliament Approves 2010 Budget', 4 January 2010, http://riskandforecast.com/post/risk-watch/yemeni-parliament-approves-2010-budget_373.html. This source cites 'estimates close to the government' who put 'the state income for 2010 at $7.6bn, while expenditure at $10.60bn'.

20 Economist Intelligence Unit, *Yemen Country Outlook*, December 2010.

21 Mareb Press, 'Central Bank Governor Announces Support for the Riyal' (in Arabic), 26 May 2010, http://www.marebpress.net/news_details.php?lng=arabic&sid=25147.

22 Saba News, 'The President Chairs Cabinet Meeting', 15 June 2010.

23 Yemen Observer, 'Yemen's Oil Revenues Increase', 14 August 2010, http://www.yobserver.com/business-and-economy/10019425.html. The episode was reminiscent of the period that followed the World Bank's announcement in 2004 that Yemen's oil supplies were likely to run out by 2012 (instead of in 2024 as had been previously anticipated). At that time, the state-owned media responded by inaccurately reporting that the Exploration Production Board had made large new discoveries of oil deposits on at least a weekly basis.

24 Some of this section was originally cited in Sarah Phillips, 'Al-Qaeda and the Struggle for Yemen', *Survival*, vol. 53, no. 1, February–March 2011, pp. 95–120.

25 World Bank, *Yemen Economic Quarterly Review*, Summer 2008.

26 For more on the increase of diesel subsidies, see Sarah Phillips, 'Cracks in the Yemeni System', *Middle East Report*, 28 July 2005.

27 Naif Hassan, 'Details of Daily Draining that Befalls Yemen', *Al-Shaari'a*, 19 January 2008.

28 Personal communication, November 2010.

29 World Bank, *Yemen Economic Quarterly Review*, Summer 2010.

30 Richard F Doner, Bryan K. Ritchie, and Dan Slater, 'Systemic Vulnerability and the Origins of Developmental States: Northeast and Southeast Asia in Comparative Perspective', *International Organization*, vol. 59, Spring 2005, p. 328.

Chapter Two

1   Brian Whitaker, *The Birth of Modern Yemen*, 2009, e-book published at http://www.al-bab.com/yemen/birthofmodernyemen.

2   Debate continues over the precise reasons for such a speedy merger but the collapse of the Soviet Union – the major patron of the South Yemeni state – and the discovery of oil in the border areas of the two states certainly created strong incentives to act on both sides of the border. International geopolitics was also an important factor, and Saddam Hussein saw Yemen as a key player in his increasing belligerence against Saudi Arabia and Kuwait. In 1989, the Arab Cooperation Council (ACC) was established between Iraq, North Yemen, Egypt and Jordan, as an explicit challenge to the Gulf Cooperation Council (GCC). Saddam supported Yemeni unification, and many argue (including Ali Salem al-Beidh), that Saddam paid money directly to President Saleh for him to rush unification. Of course, al-Beidh has other motivations for making such a claim but it is clear that Iraq's influence was strong in the process of Yemen's unification.

3   Sheila Carapico, 'Arabia Incognita: An Invitation to Arabian Peninsula Studies', in Madawi al-Rasheed and Robert Vitalis (eds), *Counter-Narratives: History, Contemporary Society, and Politics in Saudi Arabia and Yemen* (New York: Palgrave Macmillan, 2004), p.28.

4   Some prominent examples within this literature include: Abdo Baaklini, Guilain Denoeux, and Robert Springborg, *Legislative Politics in the Arab World: The Resurgence of Democratic Institutions* (Boulder, CO, and London: Lynne Rienner Publishers, 1999); Brynen, Rex Brynen, Bahgat Korany, and Paul Noble (eds), *Political Liberalization and Democratization in the Arab World: Theoretical Perspectives*, vol. 1 (Boulder, CO: Lynne Rienner Publishers, 1995); Sheila Carapico, *Civil Society in Yemen: The Political Economy of Activism in Modern Arabia* (Cambridge: Cambridge University Press, 1998); John Waterbury, 'Fortuitous By-Products', *Comparative Politics*, vol. 29, no. 3, 1997, pp. 383–402; Richard Augustus Norton (ed.), *Civil Society in the Middle East*, 2 vols. (Leiden: E.J. Brill, 1995–96).

5   These views are discussed further in Sarah Phillips, *Yemen's Democracy Experiment in Regional Perspective* (New York: Palgrave Macmillan, 2008), p. 89.

6   (Then) Prime Minister Abdul-Kareem al-Iryani addressing the Conference of Emerging Democracies in 1999. Cited in Paul Dresch, *A Modern History of Yemen* (Cambridge: Cambridge University Press, 2000), p. 212.

7   Al-Wazeer trained in Egypt, al-Hubbeishi trained in the United Kingdom. These men were both from the north and there were southerners involved in the process as well.

8   The imprint of the two existing constitutions on the draft unity constitution was relatively minor as the northern constitution explicitly banned pluralism, and the southern constitution was heavily influenced by the Soviet model.

9   The two regional groups were Shabwa-Abyan and Dhala'e-Yafa'a-Radfan.

10 Saba News, 'The President Chairs Cabinet Meeting', 15 June 2010.

11 Interview with a source close to President Saleh in Sana'a: January 2006.

12 The MCC Threshold Program is aimed at helping countries to become eligible for further assistance by demonstrating progress on selected institutional and policy reforms.

13 Interview with American diplomat, Sana'a: January 2006. This was corroborated by a source close to President Saleh in Sana'a: January 2006.

14 This was also combined with a loss of donor income from the IMF, which has been withholding $300m in concessional finance since 2002 owing to the government's failure to comply with IMF poverty reduction and growth facility reforms. Economist Intelligence Unit, *Yemen Country Profile*, 2006/2007.

15 Interview with American diplomat, Sana'a: January 2006. This was also corroborated by a source close to President Saleh in Sana'a: January 2006, and subsequently by other Western donors.

16 MOPIC (Ministry of Planning and International Cooperation), *The National Reform Agenda: A Progress Report*, October 2006, p. 1.

17 Gregory Johnsen, 'Al-Qaida In The Arabian Peninsula In Yemen: NPR', Radio Interview with Neal Conan, *Talk of the Nation*, 4 November 2010, transcript available: http://www.npr.org/templates/story/story.php?storyId=131071948. Johnsen cites an interview with 'one of the individuals who was on the plane' with President Saleh who said that the president came away from the meetings with the strong sense that 'without an al-Qaida problem in Yemen, Yemen was just one more poor country in a world of beggars'.

18 Badawi escaped from a Sana'a prison along with 22 other men affiliated with al-Qaeda in February 2006.

19 The US subsequently learned that President Saleh had also pardoned Fahd al-Quso, another of the 2006 escapees, earlier in 2007. Quso later appeared in an AQAP video threatening to attack US interests.

20 The author was in Yemen working at the National Democratic Institute at the time and was involved in a number of conversations with reformers about this issue.

21 Yacoub was later appointed as a deputy finance minister.

22 *Yemen Today* is run by Faris Sanabani, who has access to President Saleh but is not a member of the regime's inner circle.

23 For local commentary on the origins of the plan, see David MacDonald, 'The Path to Reform', *Yemen Today*, 7 March 2010, http://www.yementoday.com/go/investigations/3864.htm.

24 The Executive Committee was consciously styled after the organisation of the same name in Dubai that Sheikh Rashid championed in the 1970s. The other founding members of the group were the head of the General Investment Board, Salah Attar, and assistant to the president's Press Secretary Faris Sanabani. The Deputy Minister of MOPIC Hisham Sharaf joined later as did the head of the Customs Authority, Mohammed Zimam, Minister for Oil Amir al-Aidaroos, Minister for Justice Ghazi al-Aghbari, and President Saleh's son Ahmed Ali. While the committee is styled after its Dubai namesake, the other aspects that defined the Dubai

group – particularly the time that Sheikh Rashid devoted to educating its members at leading international universities, and his extensive funding of international study trips – are not a part of the Yemeni group's makeup.

25 Phone interview with Western donor, November 2010.

26 Phone interviews with four Western diplomats and donors, October and November 2010.

27 For a summary of the Ten Point Plan see Chatham House, 'Reform Priorities for Yemen and the 10-Point Agenda', 18 February 2010. http://www.chathamhouse.org.uk/files/16128_180210summary.pdf.

28 Phone interview with Western donor, November 2010.

29 Phone interviews with three Western diplomats and donors, October and November 2010.

30 Phone interview with Western diplomat, November 2010.

31 Interview with Western diplomat, October 2010. For an example of explicit attention the authors of the Ten Point Plan give to the international accolades the plan has received. See for example Jalal Yacoub, 'Reform Priorities for Yemen and the 10-Point Agenda', MENAP Roundtable Summary, Chatham House, February 2010, http://www.chathamhouse.org.uk/files/16128_180210summary.pdf.

32 These five priorities were to increase electricity supply, identify new sources of water, sector-based development in Aden, generate employment opportunities for Yemenis in the neighbouring GCC countries, and to increase oil and gas exploration and production. While these priorities were clearly all intended to quickly create capital, gone were the already sanitised calls for more substantive reform that were found in the original Ten Point Plan. The items removed included the reduction of diesel subsidies, tackling land dispute cases, increasing presidential involvement in the reform agenda, and increasing the rule of law. Even more than the Ten Point Plan, the Five Priorities that emerged from it were purely technical measures.

33 MOPIC, *The National Reform Agenda: A Progress Report*, October 2006.

34 Response to the questionnaire administered in Sana'a between March and July 2010.

35 Interview with a member of the Executive Committee. September 2010.

36 The passage in which it appears says: 'It is believed that these programs [i.e. the priorities for reform] will jump-start a positive process of growth and reform in Yemen, but this is only the start. Their successful execution must be followed by further efforts to expand government capacity and renewed focus on the many other challenges facing Yemen today – such as improving education and healthcare, fighting corruption, building roads, enhancing business regulation, and repairing the social safety net.'

37 USAID, '2010–2012 Yemen Country Strategy: Stabilization Through Development', 2010, http://pdf.usaid.gov/pdf_docs/PDACP572.pdf.

Chapter Three

1   The Sanhan tribe was once a member of the Bakil confederation but switched to Hashid, although it went against the rest of Hashid by supporting the royalists during the 1962–70 civil war that followed the republican revolution.

2   This figure is only a rough estimate based on interviews with a number of local experts.

3   Derek B Miller, 'Demand, Stockpiles and Social Controls: Small Arms in Yemen', Small Arms Survey, Occasional Paper no. 9, May 2003, p. 28. The methodology of how this figure calculated was based largely on educated guesswork and should be taken as indicative only.

4   Interview with a sheikh (affiliated with the GPC) who receives payments from the Department of Tribal Affairs, Sana'a, November 2004. Originally cited in Sarah Phillips, Yemen's Democracy Experiment in Regional Perspective (New York, Palgrave Macmillan, 2008).

5   Interview with a GPC member of parliament, Sana'a, October 2004. Originally cited Sarah Phillips, Yemen's Democracy Experiment in Regional Perspective.

6   Paul Dresch, The Tribal Factor in the Yemeni Crisis' in Jamal al-Suwaidi (ed.), The Yemeni War of 1994: Causes and Consequences (Emirates Centre for Strategic Studies and Research, Saqi Books, 1995), p.40.

7   Max Weber, 'The Types of Legitimate Domination', in Economy and Society, Volume 1 (Berkeley, CO, and Los Angeles, CA, University of California Press, 1978), p.236.

8   Ibid. p. 217.

9   Neopatrimonialism been most analysed with regard to leadership in Africa: William Reno, 'Clandestine Economies, Violence and States in Africa', Journal of International Affairs, vol. 53, no. 2, 2000, pp. 433–59; Patrick Chabal and Jean-Pascal Daloz, Africa Works: Disorder as Political Instrument. (London: the International African Institute, Oxford: James Currey, Bloomingdale, IL and Indianapolis, IN: Indiana University Press, 1999); Michael Bratton and Nicolas van de Walle, Democratic Experiments in Africa: Regime Transitions in Comparative Perspective (Cambridge: Cambridge University Press, 1997); Diana Cammack, 'The Logic of African Neopatrimonialism: What Role for Donors?', Development Policy Review, vol. 25, no. 5, 2007, pp. 599–614; Diana T. Cammack, E. Kanyongolo O'Neil, and F. Goloba-Mutebi, '"Big Men", Governance and Development in Neo-Patrimonial States', ODI Paper, September 2007 (London: Overseas Development Institute, 2007); Joel Migdal, Strong Societies and Weak States: State-Society Relations and State Capabilities in the Third World (Princeton, NJ: Princeton University Press, 1988).

10 Michael Bratton and Nicolas van de Walle, Democratic Experiments in Africa, pp. 63–6.

11 Anne Pitcher, Mary H. Moran, and Michael Johnston, 'Rethinking Patrimonialism and Neopatrimonialism in Africa', African Studies Review, vol. 52, no. 1, 2009, p. 127.

12 David Sebudubudu, 'Leaders, Elites and Coalitions in the Development of

Botswana', LPCRP Research Paper 2, April 2009.

13 Nasser Arrabeyee, 'Saleh Insists on Nuclear Energy for Yemen', *Yemen Observer*, 2 October 2006.

14 For more on the possibilities of development under a patrimonial political order, see Tim Kelsall and David Booth, 'Developmental Patrimonialism? Questioning the Orthodoxy on Political Governance and Economic Progress in Africa', Africa Power and Politics Programme, Overseas Development Institute, Working Paper No. 9, July 2010; Stefan Lindemann, 'Do Inclusive Elite Bargains Matter: A Research Framework for Understanding the Causes of Civil War in Sub-Saharan Africa', Crisis States Research Centre, Discussion Paper 15, February 2008.

15 While not maintaining a monopoly on legitimate force, the state does maintain a monopoly on air power and so is able, if it wishes, to deal a decisive blow to political opponents from the air, although as the Sa'da conflict and the air strikes against al-Qaeda have demonstrated there are serious political costs to this tactic.

16 See Thomas Parks and William Cole, 'Political Settlements: Implications for International Development Policy and Practice', Occasional Paper no. 02, 2010, *The Asia Foundation*, p. 29, http://www.asiafoundation.org/resources/pdfs/PoliticalSettlementsFINAL.pdf for further discussion of the various political settlements that often apply to different elite groups.

17 Glenn E. Robinson, Oliver Wilcox, Stephen Carpenter and Abdul-Ghani al-Iryani, *Yemen Corruption Assessment* (ARD Report prepared for the United States Agency for International Development – USAID) September 2006, p. 5, http://yemen.usembassy.gov/root/pdfs/reports/yemen-corruption-assessment.pdf.

18 *Ibid.*, p.5.

19 Douglass C. North, John Joseph Wallis and Barry R Weingast, *Violence and Social Orders: A Conceptual Framework for Interpreting Recorded Human History.* (Cambridge: Cambridge University Press, 2009), p. 38.

20 Participant's response to survey questionnaire administered by the DLP research team: YSP leader and former senior civil servant.

21 April Longely Alley, 'The Rules of the Game: Unpacking Patronage Politics in Yemen', *Middle East Journal*, vol. 64, no. 3, 2010, p. 394.

22 Interview with an official in a minor opposition party, Sana'a, September 2004.

23 Adel Al-Dhahab, 'Yemen's Missing Pieces for Reforms', *Yemen Post*, 14 December 2010, http://yemenpost.net/Detail123456789.aspx?ID=3&SubID=2861&MainCat=6. Ba Jammal is himself notoriously corrupt and wealthy.

24 April Longely Alley, 'The Rules of the Game: Unpacking Patronage Politics in Yemen', p. 399.

25 This has been publicly alluded to by the organisation's management. According to Brian Katulis, (then) 'chairman Abdullah Abdullah Al-Sanafani acknowledged ... that [COCA] conducts special audits requested by higher authorities, the catch phrase often used to describe the office of President Saleh'. Brian Katulis, *Yemen: Freedom House Executive Summary*, 2004, p. 9. This was originally cited in Sarah Phillips, *Yemen's Democracy Experiment in Regional*

Perspective (New York: Palgrave Macmillan, 2008), and the following chapter borrows from that work.

26 Interview with a tribal ally of President Saleh, Sana'a, December 2004.

27 Interview with local analyst (who toured the COCA vaults with a former director), Sana'a, 23 March 2005.

28 Unpublished paper by Abdul-Ghani al-Iryani, 2005, received from the author.

29 PricewaterhouseCoopers Middle East 'Tax Update', December 2009, p. 3, http://www.pwc.com/en_M1/m1/assets/document/ME-Tax-Update-Jan.pdf.

30 Heritage Foundation, 'Index of Economic Freedom', 2011 http://www.heritage.org/Index/pdf/2011/countries/yemen.pdf.

31 This has been raised in many discussions between the Yemeni government and international financial institutions.

32 Sarah Phillips, 'Evaluating Political Reform in Yemen', *Carnegie Papers, Democracy and Rule of Law Project*, no. 80, February 2007, p.12.

33 Robert Worth, 'Is Yemen the Next Afghanistan?', *New York Times*, 6 July 2010, http://www.nytimes.com/2010/07/11/magazine/11Yemen-t.html.

34 Interview with a tribal source close to President Saleh, Sana'a, December 2004.

35 Interview with two ranking officials whose positions cannot be disclosed for the purposes of anonymity, Sana'a: November 2007. After a thorough review of the revised 2008 budget, it was not possible to pinpoint exactly how this $1.75bn was distributed because there was a relatively even increase of most line items in the budget. However, crude additions amounting to a total of roughly $1.5bn can be found on the last page of the 'consolidated table of general revenue for the state at the central and local levels'. This money was allegedly to be secured through the sale of state land, liquidation of assets and international loans.

36 Benjamin Smith, 'Oil Wealth and Regime Survival in the Developing World, 1960–1999', *American Journal of Political Science*, vol. 48, no. 2, 2004, pp. 232–46. Paul Collier and Anke Hoeffler, 'Resource Rents, Governance, and Conflict', *Journal of Conflict Resolution*, vol. 49, no. 4, 2005, pp. 625–33. Gregory F Gause III, *Oil Monarchies: Domestic and Security Challenges in the Arab Gulf States* (New York: Council on Foreign Relations Press, 1994). Hazem Beblawi and Giacomo Luciani, (eds), *The Rentier State*: Volume II (London: Croom Helm, 1997). Michael Ross, 'Does Oil Hinder Democracy?', *World Politics*, vol. 53, April 2001, pp. 297–322. Terry Lynn Karl, *The Paradox of Plenty: Oil Booms and Petro-States* (Berkeley: CA and London: University of California Press, 1997).

37 David Sebudubudu, 'Leaders, Elites and Coalitions in the Development of Botswana'; Deborah Brautigam with Tania Diolle, 'Coalitions, Capitalists and Credibility: Overcoming the Crisis of Confidence at Independence in Mauritius', LECRP, April 2009.

38 Between 1972 and 1982, per capita income in the YAR increased from $135 to $420. It was not until 14 years later, in 1997, that the per capita income in the (oil producing) Republic of Yemen surpassed that of the YAR at its peak in 1982. United Nations Statistics Division, *National Accounts Main Aggregates Database*, December 2010.

39 Vote on UNSCR 678, 29 November 1990.

40 Victoria Clark, *Yemen: Dancing on the Heads of Snakes* (New Haven, CT and London: Yale University Press), 2010, p.139.

41 *Qat* is Yemen's primary cash crop and while the industry is not heavily regulated, it is widely accepted within Yemen (again, accurate official statistics do not exist) that its production and sale accounts for between 20-25 percent of the Yemeni economy. This figure was often given during fieldwork in Yemen between 2004-2008, and is corroborated by Horton, 2010. Furthermore, around 70% of *qat* is grown in three provinces: Ibb, Sana'a and Hajjah. Its distribution is tightly controlled in those governorates, which means that the taxation of *qat* producers is also concentrated in specific tribal areas, and under specific sheikhs.

42 Diplomatic cables released through Wikileaks confirm that American and British money and training that was intended for counter-terrorism have been used instead by the Yemeni regime to fight the (non-terrorism related) al-Houthi insurgency in Sa'da. United States Embassy, Sana'a, 'Yemen's Counter Terrorism Unit Stretched Thin by War Against Houthis', Diplomatic Cable, 17 December 2009. Available through Wikileaks, Reference ID 09SANAA2230, http://wikileaks.ca/cable/2009/12/09SANAA2230.html.

43 Many of the investment projects suggested by the Yemeni government are unrealistic. One of the more notable examples of this was when it triumphantly (albeit incorrectly) reported that the Bin Laden Company had commenced construction of a bridge that would link Yemen to Djbouti. The Yemeni president's assistant press secretary was particularly optimistic about the economic prospects that such a project might create for Yemen, repeatedly emphasising the many billions of dollars in revenue that he believed it would bring to the Yemeni economy, Aqeel Al-Hilali, 'Construction begins on Yemen-Djibouti Bridge', *Yemen Times*, 12 August 2009, http://www.yementimes.com/DefaultDET.aspx?i=1177&p=community&a=5.

44 April Longley and Abdul-Ghani al-Iryani, 'Fighting Brushfires with Batons: An Analysis of the Political Crisis in South Yemen', *The Middle East Institute: Policy Brief*, no. 7, February 2008.

45 Several months later al-Awadhi was temporarily excluded when he crossed a red line by publicly criticising the way that President Saleh rules Yemen in a personal and unaccountable manner.

46 The author was present in the area at the time.

47 YECO was established in the early 1970s and was initially owned by all military servicemen who contributed to its start-up capital, but was usurped and used as a commercial arm of the regime in the mid-1980s. It has business operations in a wide array of industries including basic commodities and foodstuffs, non-lethal military supplies, furniture, textiles, pharmaceuticals, agribusiness, (unlicensed) commercial fishing and real estate. Many Yemeni observers view the corporation as a vast criminal enterprise.

48 President Saleh used to be the head of YECO. Ali al-Kohali is the brother of Ahmed al-Kohali (former governor

of Aden and now the minister of parliamentary affairs), who is President Saleh's father-in-law.

49 Interview with senior government official who requested anonymity, Sana'a, March 2008.

50 Robert H. Bates, *Violence and Prosperity: The Political Economy of Development* (New York: W.W. Norton, 2001), p. 66.

51 Garrett Hardin, 'The Tragedy of the Commons', *Science*, vol. 162, no. 3859, 1968, pp. 1,243–8.

52 For a discussion of the solutions to collective action problems see Michael Laver, *Private Desires, Political Action: An Invitation to the Politics of Rational Choice* (London: Sage Books, 1997), pp. 38–67.

Chapter Four

1 Neil MacDonald and Rana Khalil, 'Report of the Assessment towards a "Whole of EU" Approach to State Building in Yemen: Addressing Fragility to Prevent State Failure', July 2009, p. 35.

2 Zaydism is a form of Shia Islam that is prevalent in the highlands of northern Yemen. It is doctrinally closer to the Sunni sects than it is to other Shia sects, particularly the *Ithna'sharis*, and is commonly referred to as the 'fifth school' of Sunni Islam.

3 Interview with source working in the security services, Sana'a, September 2008.

4 Ginny Hill, 'Riyadh Will Decide the Fate of Ali Abdullah Saleh – and of Yemen', *Guardian*, 23 March 2011, http://www.guardian.co.uk/commentisfree/2011/mar/23/ali-abdullah-saleh-riyadh-house-of-saud.

5 For example, it was widely argued that Saudi Arabia had in fact planted the parcel bombs that were intercepted on the two planes after a Saudi tip-off in October 2010. Author's conversations with ordinary Yemenis following the incident; the other common claim was that the plot was an American conspiracy. While there was little of substance to support either claim, it is indicative of the deep reservations that Yemenis hold about both Saudi Arabia and the United States.

6 Interview with senior Yemeni official, Sana'a, March 2008.

7 Gulf Research Center, 'Trans-Arabia Oil Pipelines', *Security and Terrorism Research Bulletin*, Issue no. 6, August 2007, pp. 4–6.

8 This figure was consistently reported in interviews during 2004–05 and was publicly acknowledged by the Saudi government after the death of Sheikh Abdullah in late 2007. The Saudi government confirmed that the sheikh's sons would continue to receive the monthly payment.

9 According to the Ministry of Finance, the Department of Tribal Affairs (DTA) received YR888m ($4.8m) in 2004 and was estimated to have received YR945m ($5.1m) in 2005. This seems implausibly low due to the number of sheikhs who receive funding from the government: between 4,000–5,000 people, according to a sheikh who was affiliated with the GPC and who received payments during an

interview in Sana'a in November 2004). Yemeni Ministry of Finance. *Bulletin of Government Finance Statistics,* Quarterly bulletin issued by the Ministry of Finance, issue 19, 1st quarter, 2005.

10   Interview with a source who receives regular payments from Saudi Arabia, Sana'a, November 2008.

11   Dexter Filkins, 'Letter From Yemen: After the Uprising', *The New Yorker,* 11 April 2011, http://www.newyorker. com/reporting/2011/04/11/110411fa_ fact_filkins?.

12   At the time of writing there have been six relatively discrete bouts of conflict in Sa'da, which are referred to numerically: 'the first Sa'da war', etc.

13   Interview with Yemeni security service source, February 2010.

14   Prince Sultan controls the Special Committee for Yemeni Affairs, the body that administers funds to Yemeni tribes and other Yemeni citizens.

15   United States Embassy, Sana'a, 'Yemeni Tribal Leader: For Saleh, Saudi Involvement in Sa'ada Comes Not a Moment too Soon', Diplomatic Cable, 28 December 2009. Available through WikiLeaks, Reference ID 09SANAA2279, http://wikileaks.ch/ cable/2009/12/09SANAA2279.html.

16   Interviews with three senior Western diplomats in March 2010, subsequently confirmed by a senior World Bank official. See also Christopher Boucek, 'Yemen Needs More Than Our Military Support', *Financial Times,* 31 October 2010, http://www. carnegieendowment.org/publications/ index.cfm?fa=view&id=41846. Boucek noted in 2010 that Saudi Arabia 'already gives Yemen $2bn a year'. This money greatly exceeds what Saudi Arabia pledged to contribute in formal assistance in the donor conference in

London in 2006, only a small fraction of which has been paid.

17   Oil production statistics are much more transparent than oil revenue statistics, which tend to be opaque. Ibrahim al-Nahari, sub-governor for Yemen's foreign banking operations stated that the government received $4.4bn in income from oil in 2008. Shane McGinley, 'Yemen Oil Income Falls by over Half in 2009', *Arabian Business,* 27 January 2010.

18   United States Embassy, Sana'a, 'Yemeni Tribal Leader: For Saleh, Saudi Involvement in Sa'ada Comes Not a Moment too Soon', 28 December 2009.

19   Interview with a senior Yemeni economist who participated in the survey (administered by the DLP research team) for the Developmental Leadership Program study, August 2010. This figure is in line with previous interventions by Yemen's Central Bank: in May 2010 the governor of the Central Bank stated that the bank had injected $850m from the national reserve since January 2010 to prevent the riyal from falling more than 8% against the dollar, Mareb Press, 'Central Bank Governor Announces Support for the Riyal' (in Arabic), 26 May 2010, http:// www.marebpress.net/news_details. php?lng=arabic&sid=25147.

20   Phone interviews with one Western diplomat, one Western donor and one Yemeni diplomat.

21   Interviews with members of the Yemeni cabinet and a Yemeni diplomat.

22   Al-Motamar, 'Yemen Requests $44.5 Billion from Donors up to Year 2015', 27 February 2010, http://www. almotamar.net/en/7312.htm.

23   Ian Black, 'Yemen Pledges to Reform and Wins Support for Fight against

Al-Qaeda', *Guardian*, 27 January 2010.

24 Interview with participant in the survey administered by the DLP research team, mid-2010.

25 These figures are according to Assistant to the President for Homeland Security and Counterterrorism John Brennan, speaking on 17 December 2010.

26 Jon Bennett, Debi Duncan, Ines Rothmann, Sushila Zeitlyn and Ginny Hill, 'DFID Country Programme Evaluation, Yemen', *British Department of International Development Evaluation Report EV706*, February 2010, p. 10, http://www.dfid.gov.uk/Documents/ publications1/evaluation/cnty-prog-eval-ye.pdf.

Chapter Five

1 Figures vary somewhat due to the presence of 'ghost soldiers', that is, names that collect a salary but do not really exist.

2 The fact that both Yahya and 'Ammar are 'deputy commanders' does not mean that they are subservient to anyone else in their organisation. The official commander of the National Security Bureau, for example, is Ali al-Ansi, but the power is with 'Ammar. It is very often the case that ministers are less powerful than their deputy ministers, because the deputies have been appointed on the basis of the ties to President Saleh.

3 He was previously the head of the Presidential Guard before the president's nephew Tariq assumed the position.

4 Mohammed Ali Muhsin is a member of the shiekhly Sanhan family that dominates Bayt al-Ahmar (Maqsa'). He is related to President Saleh's family by marriage, and is not related to Ali Muhsin.

5 Personal communication with Yemeni security source, March 2011.

6 Confirmed during several interviews with people close to Ali Muhsin.

7 The house stands out on the way to the airport; it is also his military base.

8 Interview with source close to members of the Sanhan tribe. Date and place withheld for reasons of anonymity.

9 Until about 1995, Ali al-Ansi, the director of the Office of the President was also considered part of this 'kitchen cabinet' but he no longer enjoys the same level of access as his deputy Abdo Burji. Al-Ansi was trained in the police academy in Egypt and returned to Yemen about one month after President Saleh came to power. A close confidant of President Saleh at the time confirmed in an interview that Saleh was looking for someone with good handwriting, and that al-Ansi got the job on this basis. Sana'a, March 2010.

10 The International Crisis Group also comments on the difficulties of trying to document the widespread views about the elite politics that may be at least partly fuelling the Sa'da wars, and cites a Western diplomat as saying that the Sa'da wars are a 'poisoned chalice given to Ali Muhsin', International Crisis Group. 'Yemen: Defusing the Saada Time Bomb', *Middle East Report*, no. 86, 27 May 2009, p. 15,

http://www.crisisgroup.org/~/media/Files/Middle East North Africa/Iran Gulf/Yemen/o86 Yemen Defusing the Saada Time Bomb.ashx. Within Yemen, this contention is seldom questioned, and was confirmed in private conversations with numerous military and political elites that are connected to Ali Muhsin.

11 Al-Jazeera, 6 November 2009. For English language commentary see: http://blogs.aljazeera.net/middle-east/2009/11/16/yemens-complex-reality; http://yementribune.com/blog/?p=1111.

12 The grievances were also related to the encroachment of government-supported Salafi Islam in the strongly Zaydi area.

13 Interview with a source close to President Saleh, Sana'a, April 2007. This was later corroborated in an interview with a source within the military.

14 Interview with a source with access to President Saleh, Sana'a, October 2009.

15 Erica Frantz and Natasha Ezrow, *The Politics of Dictatorship: Institutions and Outcomes in Authoritarian Regimes* (Boulder, CO: Lynne Rienner, 2011).

16 This story was conveyed during an interview with a Sanhan insider. All other details are withheld to maintain the anonymity of those present.

17 It is unknown whether this was written down.

18 Deputy Chief of Staff Ahmed Faraj was also killed in the crash; he was a supporter of Ali Muhsin but it is unclear whether he also spoke out against the possibility of Ahmed Ali coming to power.

19 For example, some units commanded by officers loyal to Ali Muhsin had to surrender their tanks to Republican Guard units.

20 Political analyst Abdul-Ghani al-Iryani has made this point in a number of conference presentations.

21 While a generation is usually understood to be 25 years, in the Yemeni context it is significantly less than this – about 17 or 18 years.

22 Rashad Sharabi, 'Study Centre Led By Ali Muhsin Combines al-Iryani, al-Ra'i, al-Maqaleh and Others', *Mareb Press* (in Arabic), 8 September 2007, http://www.marebpress.net/news_details.php?lng=arabic&sid=7520.

23 The author was in Yemen conducting fieldwork at the time.

24 One recent example of this was after the end of the Sixth Sa'da war (February 2010), it was nearly announced that President Saleh's son, Ahmed, would be named the general commander of the armed forces. This would have meant that Ali Muhsin would have effectively been under Ahmed Ali's command. When Ahmed travelled to Saudi Arabia to meet with King Abdullah, the official media announced that the king had met with General Commander Ahmed Ali Abdullah Saleh. This promotion has not been mentioned again and it appears that the inner circle exercised its veto on this occasion.

25 Sadiq does not wield the level of influence that his father did and his brothers Hameed and Hussein are also very prominent leaders in the Hashid confederation.

26 Bayt al-Ahmar and the Hashid elite maintain very strong leverage over the president but not to the extent of holding a veto over him.

27 Some Yemenis will argue that Hameed's brother, Hussein, is in fact the more astute of the two because he remains seen first and foremost as a Hashid tribesman, whereas Hameed

plays to many different – some say competing – audiences.

28 As noted above in Chapter 4, Hameed and his brothers collectively receive $800,000 as a monthly stipend from Saudi Arabia since their father's death in late December 2007. The author was not able to determine the formula by which this money is divided between the al-Ahmar brothers.

29 Estimates vary considerably on the number of fighters he rallied but most estimates put it at a maximum of 3,000 but probably less.

30 At the official launch of the committee, the group's name was changed from 'The Virtue Committee' to 'The Committee for the Propagation of Virtue', to be more in line with its Saudi Arabian counterpart 'The Committee for the Propagation of Virtue and Prevention of Vice'.

31 Mareb Press, 'President Saleh Establishes Religious Reference Committee for All Issues and Political Forces', 7 September 2010 (in Arabic), http://www.marebpress.net/news_details.php?lng=arabic&sid=27366.

32 Holger Albrecht, 'The Political Economy of Reform in Yemen: Privatisation, Investment, and the Yemeni Business Climate', *Asien Afrika Lateinamerika*, vol. 30, 2002, p. 143. Albrecht cites a study carried out in 1988 (prior to unification), which said that of the 32 government officials surveyed, 21 already owned personal private enterprises and eight were planning to establish one for themselves. See Omar Osman Mohammed, 'Socio-Cultural and Managerial Behaviour of Yemeni Entrepreneurs', *Orient*, vol. 36, no. 2, 1995, p. 299.

Chapter Six

1 This profile of the JMP draws on an unpublished paper written for Yemen's National Democratic Institute: Sarah Phillips and Murad Zafir, 'Baseline Assessment of the Joint Meeting Parties (JMP) Coalition in Yemen', unpublished, 2007.

2 Jeb Boone, 'Yemen's President Plays the Trusted Al-Qaida Card', *guardian.co.uk*, 7 March 2011, http://www.guardian.co.uk/commentisfree/2011/mar/07/yemen-al-qaida-salih-islamic-terrorists.

3 These figures were obtained during the research for Phillips and Zafir, 'Baseline Assessment of the Joint Meeting Parties'.

4 Sayyid status is not formally required to hold a leadership position, and the party's membership extends beyond this narrow group.

5 Participant's response to survey administered by the DLP research team: JMP leader and former senior civil servant.

6 To see the agreement, see National Democratic Institute 'Report on the 2006 Presidential and Local Council Elections in the Republic of Yemen' p. 23. http://www.ndi.org/files/2152_ye_report_elections_042407.pdf.

7 Mareb Press, 'To Turn it Into a Personal Project [i.e. for personal benefit]…' (in Arabic), 3 June 2010.

8 Participant's response to survey administered by the DLP research team: JMP (Islah) leader.

9 Abigail Fielding-Smith, 'Kingmaker Seeks Stable, Developed Yemen', *Financial Times*, 25 March 2011.

10 Sharon Beatty, Ahmed No'man al-Madhaji and Renaud Detalle, 'Yemeni NGOs and Quasi NGOs, Analysis and Directory, Part 1: Analysis' (Sana'a, Republic of Yemen: no publisher listed, May 1996), p. 20. Kiren Aziz Chaudhry, 'The Price of Wealth: Business and State in Labor Remittance and Oil Economies', *International Organization*, vol. 43 no. 1, 1989, pp. 133–4.

11 Sheila Carapico, *Civil Society in Yemen: The Political Economy of Activism in Modern Arabia* (Cambridge: Cambridge University Press, 1998), p. 38.

12 The following description of the GPC borrows from Sarah Phillips, *Yemen's Democracy Experiment in Regional Perspective* (New York: Palgrave Macmillan, 2008), pp. 50–51

13 He believed that they were either 'minor and temporary' or 'serious but temporary'.

14 While 'leadership' was one of nine specific options listed in the survey administered by the DLP research team, we have also taken into account the participant's statements in the semi-structured interviews that followed, and if they clearly emphasised leadership in the latter part of their assessment, their response has been included in this category.

15 Of the 17% of participants (11 people) who did not nominate agential factors, all but one was from the GPC, the other was from the Ba'ath Party, which left its alliance with the GPC to join the JMP in 2008. One participant also refused to answer the question regarding the causes of Yemen's problems.

16 United States Embassy, Sana'a, 'Yemeni Tribal Leader: For Saleh, Saudi Involvement in Sa'ada Comes Not a Moment too Soon'.

17 The Majlis al-Shura is a body of 111 members all appointed by the president that, while technically a part of the executive branch, serves more as an advisory board to the executive, although it was granted several legislative powers in 2001.

Chapter seven

1 The first protests in Yemen were held the day after the Tunisian president fled the country.

2 President Saleh's supporters displayed placards with the words 'Burghulis out' – a derogatory term for workers and technocrats in the surrounds of Ta'izz. In trying to blame the people of Ta'izz for the rising unrest, Saleh was inciting the regime's traditional tribal heartland against the latent commercial elite.

3 On 1 March 2011, President Saleh stated: 'I am going to reveal a secret … There is an operations room in Tel Aviv with the aim of destabilising the Arab world. The operations room is in Tel Aviv and run by the White House … Regrettably those (opposition figures) are sitting day and night with the American ambassador where they hand him reports and he gives them instructions.' Cited in Associated

Press, 'US and Israel Behind Unrest: Yemeni Leader', 2 March 2011. http://www.news.smh.com.au/breaking-news-world/us-and-israel-behind-unrest-yemeni-leader-20110302-1bde5.html.

4   Personal communication with a Yemeni who was present at Zindani's house at the time, February 2011.

5   Personal communication with two people who were present at the time, March 2011.

6   Personal communication with source close to the Sanhan tribe, April 2011.

7   No representatives of the protesters were involved in these closed-door negotiations.

8   Abu Dhabi Television, Interview with President Saleh, 10 January 2010. Transcript available: http://www.presidentsaleh.gov.ye/shownews.php?lng=ar&_nsid=7991&_newsctgry=4&_newsyr=2010 (in Arabic).

9   Dubai Sports Channel, Interview with President Saleh, 18 December 2009. Transcript available: http://www.presidentsaleh.gov.ye/shownews.php?lng=ar&_nsid=7962&_newsctgry=4&_newsyr=2009 (in Arabic).

10 Shane McGinley, 'Yemen Oil Income Falls by over Half in 2009', Arabian Business, 27 January 2010.

11 Hussein Leswaas, 'The Role of the President in the Factional Conflict in Saudi Arabia', al-Masdar, 4 November 2010, http://www.almasdaronline.com/index.php?page=news&article-section=10&news_id=12872 (in Arabic).

12 United States Embassy, Sana'a, 'Yemeni Tribal Leader: For Saleh, Saudi Involvement in Sa'ada Comes Not a Moment too Soon', Diplomatic Cable, 28 December 2009. Available through WikiLeaks, Reference ID 09SANAA2279, http://wikileaks.ch/cable/2009/12/09SANAA2279.html.

13 Being significantly older than the average Yemeni citizen, the political elite are likely to remember the level of instability before President Saleh came to power in 1978, and the fact that in the nine months before he came to office the previous two north Yemeni presidents had died violently.

Conclusions

1   Stephen Cohen, The Idea of Pakistan (Washington DC: Brookings Institution Press, 2004), cited in Ahmed Rashid, Descent into Chaos: The United States and the Failure of Nation Building in Pakistan, Afghanistan, and Central Asia (London: Penguin Books, 2008) p. 291.

2   Paul Richter, 'Hillary Clinton Urges Yemen to "Take Ownership" of its Problems', Los Angeles Times, 27 January 2010, http://articles.latimes.com/2010/jan/27/world/la-fg-yemen28-2010jan28.

3   Barack Obama, 'President Obama's Remarks on Violence in Yemen', The White House: Office of the Press Secretary, 18 March 2011, http://www.america.gov/st/texttrans-english/2011/March/20110318130339suo.8830334.html.

4   Agence France Presse, 'US Says Post-Saleh Yemen Would Pose "Real Problem"', 27 March 2011, http://www.france24.com/en/20110327-us-says-post-saleh-yemen-would-pose-real-problem.

5 Cited in Associated Press, 'US and Israel Behind Unrest: Yemeni Leader', 2 March 2011. http://www.news.smh. com.au/breaking-news-world/us-and-israel-behind-unrest-yemeni-leader-20110302-1bde5.html.

6 Personal communication, October 2010.

7 The Community Livelihoods Project for Yemen states: 'it will be important to focus on the most vulnerable areas, where stabilization needs are greatest, where interventions can have significant impact, where conflict drivers can be mitigated, and where government presence and legitimacy can be reinvigorated'. USAID, 'Community Livelihoods Project: Project Guidelines', RFA 279-10-006, 2010, p. 6.

8 The World Food Programme reported in March 2010 that '61.4% of all food-insecure and 66.9% of severely food-insecure people in the country are concentrated in 5 of [Yemen's] 19 governorates (Al-Hodieda, Amran, Hajja, Ibb and Taiz)'. World Food Programme, *Comprehensive Food Security Survey: Republic of Yemen*, March 2010, p. 40. Only one of these governorates, 'Amran, is included in the eight governorates that are targeted by USAID's livelihoods programme.

9 Aden may be at least a partial exception to this, although it was the site of the USS *Cole* bombing in 2000 and the Gold Mohur Hotel bombing in 1993.

10 Oil and gas are extracted from reserves in Marib and Shabwa but few goods are produced in these areas.

11 USAID, 'Community Livelihoods Project: Project Guidelines', p. 6. For further discussion of AQAP's narrative in these areas see Sarah Phillips, 'Al-Qaeda and the Struggle for Yemen', *Survival*, vol. 53, no. 1, February–March 2011, pp. 95–120.

12 The same is true for technocrats within the Yemeni government, who often refer to the Ten Point Plan as an effort to 'stop the bleeding', and prioritise the parts of the package that would have a fast visible impact.

Adelphi books are published eight times a year by Routledge Journals, an imprint of Taylor & Francis, 4 Park Square, Milton Park, Abingdon, Oxfordshire OX14 4RN, UK.

A subscription to the institution print edition, ISSN 1944-5571, includes free access for any number of concurrent users across a local area network to the online edition, ISSN 1944-558X

2011 Annual Adelphi Subscription Rates			
Institution	£491	$864 USD	€726
Individual	£230	$391 USD	€312
Online only	£442	$778 USD	€653

Dollar rates apply to subscribers outside Europe. Euro rates apply to all subscribers in Europe except the UK and the Republic of Ireland where the pound sterling price applies. All subscriptions are payable in advance and all rates include postage. Journals are sent by air to the USA, Canada, Mexico, India, Japan and Australasia. Subscriptions are entered on an annual basis, i.e. January to December. Payment may be made by sterling cheque, dollar cheque, international money order, National Giro, or credit card (Amex, Visa, Mastercard).

For more information, visit our website: **http://www.informaworld.com/ adelphipapers.**

For a complete and up-to-date guide to Taylor & Francis journals and books publishing programmes, and details of advertising in our journals, visit our website: **http://www.informaworld.com.**

Ordering information:
USA/Canada: Taylor & Francis Inc., Journals Department, 325 Chestnut Street, 8th Floor, Philadelphia, PA 19106, USA. **UK/Europe/Rest of World:** Routledge Journals, T&F Customer Services, T&F Informa UK Ltd., Sheepen Place, Colchester, Essex, CO3 3LP, UK.

Advertising enquiries to:
USA/Canada: The Advertising Manager, Taylor & Francis Inc., 325 Chestnut Street, 8th Floor, Philadelphia, PA 19106, USA. Tel: +1 (800) 354 1420. Fax: +1 (215) 625 2940.

UK/Europe/Rest of World: The Advertising Manager, Routledge Journals, Taylor & Francis, 4 Park Square, Milton Park, Abingdon, Oxfordshire OX14 4RN, UK. Tel: +44 (0) 20 7017 6000. Fax: +44 (0) 20 7017 6336.

The print edition of this journal is printed on ANSI conforming acid-free paper by Bell & Bain, Glasgow, UK.